MAPPING YOUR TRAVELS
& RELOCATION

About the Authors

Maritha Pottenger (California) has taught astrology worldwide for more than twenty-five years. Winner of the Best Lecturer award from the American Federation of Astrologers, she has been a guest speaker at the International Society for Astrological Research conferences and other astrology-related events.

Kris Brandt Riske, M.A. (Arizona) is a professional, certified astrologer. She serves on the board of the National Council for Geocosmic Research and has written numerous articles for popular astrology magazines. She is also the author of *Mapping Your Future* and *Mapping Your Money*.

To Write to the Authors

If you wish to contact the authors or would like more information about this book, please write to the authors in care of Llewellyn Worldwide and we will forward your request. Both the authors and publisher appreciate hearing from you and learning of your enjoyment of this book and how it has helped you. Llewellyn Worldwide cannot guarantee that every letter written to the authors can be answered, but all will be forwarded. Please write to:

Maritha Pottenger & Kris Brandt Riske, M.A.
⁒ Llewellyn Worldwide
2143 Wooddale Drive, Dept. 0-7387-0665-6
Woodbury, MN 55125-2989, U.S.A.
Please enclose a self-addressed stamped envelope for reply,
or $1.00 to cover costs. If outside U.S.A., enclose
international postal reply coupon.

Many of Llewellyn's authors have websites with additional information and resources. For more information, please visit our website at
http://www.llewellyn.com.

MAPPING YOUR TRAVELS & RELOCATION

Finding the Best Place for You

Maritha Pottenger
& Kris Brandt Riske, M.A.

Llewellyn Publications
Woodbury, MN

First Edition
First Printing, 2005

Book design by Donna Burch
Cover art © Digital Vision and Digital Stock
Cover design by Kevin R. Brown
Edited by Andrea Neff
Llewellyn is a registered trademark of Llewellyn Worldwide, Ltd.

Chart wheels were produced by the Kepler program by permission of Cosmic Patterns Software, Inc. (www.AstroSoftware.com)

Library of Congress Cataloging-in-Publication Data

Pottenger, Maritha.
    Mapping your travels & relocation : finding the best place for you / Maritha Pottenger & Kris Brandt Riske.—1st ed.
        p.   cm.
    ISBN 0-7387-0665-5
      1. Astrology. 2. Moving, Household—Miscellanea. 3. Travel—Miscellanea. I. Title : Mapping your travels and relocation. II. Riske, Kris Brandt. III. Title.

    BF1729.M68P68 2005
    133.5—dc22   2005044110

Llewellyn Publications
A Division of Llewellyn Worldwide, Ltd.
2143 Wooddale Drive, Dept. 0-7387-0665-6
Woodbury, MN 55125-2989, U.S.A.
www.llewellyn.com

Printed in the United States of America

Other Books by Maritha Pottenger

Astrology: The Next Step

Easy Astrology Guide

Healing with the Horoscope

Past Lives, Future Choices: The Astrology of Reincarnation

Planets on the Move: The Astrology of Relocation
(with Zipporah Dobyns)

Unveiling Your Future: Progressions Made Easy
(with Zipporah Dobyns)

Your Starway to Love: The Astrology of Romance

Chiron: Teacher, Healer, Idealist and Tragic Hero

Healing Mother-Daughter Relationships with Astrology
(with Zipporah Dobyns)

Other Books and Articles by Kris Brandt Riske, M.A.

Mapping Your Future

Mapping Your Money

Llewellyn's Moon Sign Book
(contributor, 2002–2007)

Llewellyn's Sun Sign Book
(contributor, 2007)

Llewellyn's Starview Almanac
(contributor, 2005–2006)

Civilization Under Attack
(contributor)

Astrometeorology: Planetary Power in Weather Forecasting

Contents

Charts

All chart data for celebrities and public figures comes from AstroDatabank (www.astrodatabank.com).
All chart data for anonymous case studies comes from client files.

Introduction

People are on the move every day, whether a few blocks or miles to a new home, or cross-country to pursue exciting new opportunities.

If a move is in your future, *Mapping Your Travels & Relocation* will give you valuable information about what to expect at your new location. This book is also a terrific resource for students weighing various college options, people looking toward retirement, and those who have been offered a job in another location. Maybe you've always been attracted to a specific part of the country or world, and wonder if it's truly the right move for you.

If you feel that your life lacks an important component or that your goals aren't being fulfilled in your current location, it might be time to consider new horizons. In Iowa, Texas, California, Vermont, or one of the other forty-six states, you might have more success in realizing romance, a loving partnership, greater financial security, improved health, a more active spiritual life, an entertaining social life, more public recognition, greater career success, and more.

Astrology can help you in all these situations because changing your location changes your horoscope (somewhat). Just as different people stimulate the various facets of your personality as well as your interests, skills, and talents, various geographic locations bring out different sides of your nature.

By looking at your birth chart (horoscope) as it appears in different locations, you can see which aspects of your personality are most emphasized in which areas. Then you can choose a locale that puts certain qualities in high focus and/or minimizes others.

Is there a catch? Well, there are two caveats.

Caveat one is that your options are more limited if you live in the United States and have no interest in moving to another country. The continental United States, which spans about 3,000 miles and four time zones, narrows the potential locations where you can maximize the energy represented in your birth chart. If the world is your destination, however, your choices encompass the entire spectrum of your birth chart.

Suppose, for example, that the shy, self-critical, hard-working sign of Virgo is a strong influence in your birth chart. You can probably move to a location within the United States that emphasizes fiery, dramatic, fun-loving Leo or diplomatic, affable, sociable Libra. But adventurous, confident, extroverted, expressive Sagittarius is probably out of your reach, because such a move could take you to another country or the middle of the ocean.

Caveat two is that there are no perfect birth charts because there are no perfect people. The birth chart reflects your personality, including your strengths and weaknesses. You can choose to move to an area that accentuates certain strengths, but it's impossible to eliminate all the challenges, because they, in part, represent life lessons experienced in the outer world as well as within your very being, your soul.

Every chart is a mixture of harmony and conflict. Though it's possible to emphasize the positives in one geographic area, there is no location that erases all conflict and personal challenges. But by picking and choosing from various locations, you increase the chance to strengthen certain characteristics and fulfill your potential, while minimizing those you feel are less desirable.

Like moving, life is a journey to be embraced and experienced!

1
Astrology: The Basics

Before you begin mapping your moves, it's important to know the astrological basics. It will help you better understand yourself, as well as how your birth chart (horoscope), which represents you, responds in various locations around the country or the world.

In one location you might excel at artistic endeavors or relationships, and in another you might find financial or career success. Which is which is determined by your chart and where you choose to live or visit—and your life priorities and ambitions.

Although every chart is composed of the same four main elements, each is as unique as the person it represents. What sets you apart from everyone else is the specific date, time, and location of your birth.

Every chart has twelve signs, one of which is your Sun sign; ten planets; and twelve houses, each of which represents certain areas of life, such as career, money, and family. Aspects (geometric angles), the fourth major factor in the chart, combine the energy of two or more planets.

Before reading further, calculate your chart (or a friend's or relative's—someone you know well) using the CD-ROM in the back of this book. Then you can easily identify each part of the chart as you learn the basics used by astrologers.

Bill Clinton's chart (chart 1) is used in this chapter to illustrate the basic astrological techniques, which you can then apply to your own chart.

Planets

There are ten planets (to make it easy, astrologers refer to the Sun and Moon as planets): the Sun, Moon, Mercury, Venus, Mars, Jupiter, Saturn, Uranus, Neptune, and Pluto. Find each of the planets in Bill Clinton's chart and your own chart by using the list below to identify the glyphs that represent them, and read about their essential characteristics (keywords). You'll learn more about the planets and their individual meanings in chapter 2.

Planet	*Glyph*	*Keywords*
Sun	☉	Confidence, strength, leadership
Moon	☽	Emotions, nurturing, domestic
Mercury	☿	Communication, thinking, observing
Venus	♀	Money, harmony, love, cooperation
Mars	♂	Active, dynamic, pioneering, impulsive
Jupiter	♃	Expansive, fortunate, generous
Saturn	♄	Responsible, thrifty, patient, conservative
Uranus	♅	Independent, eccentric, humanitarian
Neptune	♆	Idealistic, deceptive, compassionate
Pluto	♇	Intensity, transformation, power

Notice that the keywords describe what each planet represents in your (and every) chart, but not the ways in which the characteristics manifest. For example, even though Mercury represents communication in every chart, not everyone has the same communication style. Some people grab every opportunity to speak in public, while others shy away from it. Some people are terse, and others are tactful.

The first factor that differentiates your Mercury (and each of the other planets) from someone else's is its sign placement.

Signs

There are twelve signs in the zodiac, and each is 30° (12 x 30° = 360°, or a perfect circle). You probably know your Sun sign (determined by the month and date of your birth), as

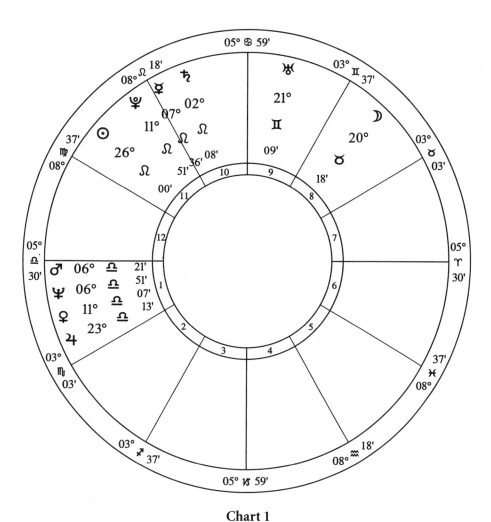

Chart 1
Bill Clinton, Birth Chart
August 19, 1946 / Hope, AR / 8:51 AM CST +6:00
Placidus Houses

do most people. Just as your Sun was traveling through a specific sign of the zodiac at the time of your birth, so were the other nine planets.

People born under the same Sun sign have some similar personality characteristics, likes and dislikes, interests, and motivations, but each is an individual. So even though you have certain basic drives in common with those who share your Sun sign, the sign placement of each of the other nine planets is one factor that differentiates you from millions of other people.

Someone with action-oriented Mars in Leo, for example, is outgoing and energetic, while the person with Mars in Taurus is thorough and determined. Action is still action—the sign placement describes how it manifests, how the individual directs the energy.

Find Mars in Bill Clinton's chart (left side, middle). Notice that next to the glyph for Mars (♂) is 06° ♎ 21'. This means Mars was in Libra, at 6 degrees, 21 minutes of that sign, when he was born. Using the list below, identify which sign each of the ten planets occupies in your chart.

Aries	♈	Taurus	♉	Gemini	♊	Cancer	♋
Leo	♌	Virgo	♍	Libra	♎	Scorpio	♏
Sagittarius	♐	Capricorn	♑	Aquarius	♒	Pisces	♓

Signs also are divided into categories called elements and modes. The four elements are fire, earth, air, and water, and the three modes are cardinal, fixed, and mutable. Each sign is associated with one element and one mode.

Signs in the same element are compatible, but those with the same mode often clash. The earth signs, for example, are all practical, but each acts according to its mode: Capricorn (cardinal earth) initiates tasks, Taurus (fixed earth) focuses its energy on one task at a time, and Virgo (mutable earth) can handle multiple tasks at one time.

Keywords for the elements are as follows:

- Fire—Action, enthusiasm, courage, spontaneity
- Earth—Conservative, reserved, dependable, practical
- Air—Curious, intellectual, perceptive, alert
- Water—Sensitive, intuitive, receptive, subjective

Here are keywords for the modes:

- Cardinal—Initiative, drive, motivation
- Fixed—Determined, stable, persistent
- Mutable—Flexible, changeable, versatile

When the elements and modes are combined, the keywords for the signs are as follows:

- Aries—Initiative, enthusiasm, ambitious, impatient
- Taurus—Thorough, thrifty, steadfast, materialistic
- Gemini—Adaptable, curious, intellectual, scattered
- Cancer—Emotional, domestic, nurturing, clinging
- Leo—Dynamic, generous, determined, egocentric
- Virgo—Practical, detail-oriented, analytical, worrisome
- Libra—Partnership, considerate, refined, indecisive
- Scorpio—Intense, intuitive, determined, secretive
- Sagittarius—Adventuresome, generous, optimistic, blunt
- Capricorn—Ambitious, patient, responsible, bossy
- Aquarius—Independent, freedom-loving, inventive, erratic
- Pisces—Sensitive, sympathetic, intuitive, impractical

When the keywords for the planets and signs are combined, the person represented by the chart begins to emerge. For example, by using keywords for Mars and Libra, Bill Clinton can be described as active and impulsive in partnerships. With Mercury in Leo, his communication style is dynamic and confident.

Now do the same with your chart. Using the keywords for the planets and signs, blend the nature of the two to create a phrase describing each planet in your chart.

Each sign is linked with a specific planet, known as its ruler. For example, Mars rules Aries, the Moon rules Cancer, and the Sun rules Leo. Some planets rule two signs, and some signs are ruled by two planets. Although not exactly the same, a sign and its ruling planet have similar characteristics. Aquarius is independent, as is its ruling planet, Uranus, and the Moon and Cancer are nurturing and protective. Planets are more comfortable in the signs they rule because they can more freely express their energy.

Signs, Planets, Elements, and Modes

Signs	Ruling Planet(s)	Element	Mode
Aries ♈	Mars ♂	Fire	Cardinal
Taurus ♉	Venus ♀	Earth	Fixed
Gemini ♊	Mercury ☿	Air	Mutable
Cancer ♋	Moon ☽	Water	Cardinal
Leo ♌	Sun ☉	Fire	Fixed
Virgo ♍	Mercury ☿	Earth	Mutable
Libra ♎	Venus ♀	Air	Cardinal
Scorpio ♏	Mars ♂, Pluto ♇	Water	Fixed
Sagittarius ♐	Jupiter ♃	Fire	Mutable
Capricorn ♑	Saturn ♄	Earth	Cardinal
Aquarius ♒	Saturn ♄, Uranus ♅	Air	Fixed
Pisces ♓	Jupiter ♃, Neptune ♆	Water	Mutable

Houses

Every chart is divided into twelve pie-shaped pieces called houses. The houses, which are numbered one through twelve, represent areas of life, such as money, family, travel, and education, and symbolize the "location" where each planet finds its strongest outlet for self-expression.

Here are the areas of life associated with each house:

- First house—Self
- Second house—Personal resources/money
- Third house—Communication
- Fourth house—Home and family
- Fifth house—Romance, children, speculation
- Sixth house—Work, service, health
- Seventh house—Relationships, marriage

- Eighth house—Joint resources, lenders
- Ninth house—Higher education, travel
- Tenth house—Career, status
- Eleventh house—Friends, groups, goals
- Twelfth house—Introspection, health

Continuing with Bill Clinton's chart, Mars in Libra in the first house can be described as self-directed, active, and impulsive in partnerships. Mercury in Leo is in the eleventh house, so Clinton is a dynamic, confident communicator with friends and groups, and clearly defines and pursues his life goals.

Now add the house keywords to the descriptions of your planet/sign combinations.

The beginning of each house is called a cusp, and each cusp has a sign and its degrees and minutes. For example, 3° ♐ 37' on the cusp of Bill Clinton's third house is 3 degrees, 37 minutes of Sagittarius. The planet ruling the sign on the cusp also rules that house. Because Sagittarius is the sign on Clinton's third-house cusp, the ruling planet is Jupiter, which will influence his thinking and communication. These planetary rulerships are especially important in assessing empty houses—those that contain no planets—which every chart has because there are ten planets and twelve houses.

Four of the house cusps have a special designation and are collectively called the angles. The first-house cusp is the Ascendant; the fourth-house cusp is the IC *(Imum Coeli);* the seventh-house cusp is the Descendant; and the tenth-house cusp is the Midheaven (MC). The angles are sensitive points that reveal additional information about a person's personality (Ascendant), home and family (IC), relationships (Descendant), and career and status (Midheaven). They are especially important in determining which locations will have a potentially positive or negative effect, whether you're considering relocating or assessing your current or birth location in terms of life goals and interests.

Aspects

Aspects are the fourth major chart component. An aspect is a geometric angle, such as 90° or 120°, that connects the energy of two or more planets or angles. Because the aspect serves as a link, each planet or angle involved in the aspect takes on some of the characteristics of the other. The result is favorable or unfavorable, depending upon the planets involved, the specific aspect, and how it is used.

Aspects are divided into two categories: hard and soft (also often referred to as difficult and easy). Soft aspects indicate energy that flows with little effort, which can be a plus or a minus. For example, if learning is easy, you might not push yourself to excel and live up to your full potential. The soft aspects are the sextile, trine, and conjunction (depending upon the planets involved in the conjunction).

Hard aspects are motivators that yield rewards once you learn to manage them. For example, career achievements might be slow in coming, but if you stick with it, you can rise higher than someone who has only soft aspects. The hard aspects are the square, opposition, and conjunction (depending upon the planets involved in the conjunction).

Aspects modify the way the planets and angles express themselves. For example, if your Sun is in restless Gemini and in square aspect to conservative Saturn, you are less outgoing than someone who has fun-loving Jupiter trine the Sun. Conversely, if your Sun is in serious Capricorn and trine Jupiter, you are more easygoing and adventuresome than a true Capricorn.

Few aspects are exact, and all have a range, or orb, of effectiveness. The closer the aspect, the stronger it is. In this book, the orbs for the major birth chart aspects are 8° for all but the sextile and inconjunct, which have orbs of 6°. For example, two planets at 18°00' Leo form an exact conjunction. Planets at 9°00' Leo and 16°30' Leo are also conjunct, because they are separated by 7°30' (which is within the 8° orb).

The major, or strongest, aspects are listed here. There are many minor aspects used by astrologers, but the six major ones provide enough basic information to accurately assess birth chart potential.

Aspect	Glyph	Degrees	Significance
Sextile	✶	60°	Opportunity
Trine	△	120°	Ease, luck
Square	□	90°	Conflict, action
Opposition	☍	180°	Separation
Conjunction	☌	0°	Intensity
Inconjunct	⚻	150°	Separation

If you want to identify the aspects yourself, the simplest way is to use the elements and modes. Planets in the same element are trine each other. For example, the water signs—Cancer, Scorpio, and Pisces—are each 120° apart. Sextile signs are those 60°, or two signs, apart, and in complementary elements; fire signs are sextile air signs, and earth signs are sextile water signs.

Planets in square (90°) or opposition (180°) aspect to each other share the same mode—cardinal, fixed, or mutable. For example, Aries is square Cancer and Capricorn, and is opposite Libra.

Conjunction (0°) planets have the same element and mode.

Inconjunct (150°) planets have different elements and modes.

Bill Clinton's Mars is conjunct Neptune and Venus, forming what astrologers call a stellium (three or more planets in conjunction), and is sextile another stellium composed of Saturn, Mercury, and Pluto. This is a powerful planetary configuration that involves six of the ten planets. Using the keywords, Clinton's first-house Mars conjunct Venus and Neptune shows he invests considerable time and energy in relationships, and can at times deceive or be deceived; this stellium also reflects his compassionate and charming nature. Mars, Venus, and Neptune sextile Mercury reinforces his ability as a strong, energetic, and smooth communicator and one who has the opportunity to get involved in groups and to form friendships with people who can advance his goals.

Now identify the aspects in your chart and, using the aspect keywords, expand the descriptive phrases of your planets.

Relocated Charts

When calculating your chart (using the CD-ROM that accompanies this book), you entered the city of your birth, which the software then translated into the longitude and latitude for that location.

Like a chart, the Earth's equator is a 360° circle. Longitude is defined by longitudinal "lines" that run from the North Pole to the South Pole, bisecting the equator. Greenwich, England, was designated 0° longitude in 1884, and also is the starting point for the world's time zones. Longitude is measured from 0° to 180° west and from 0° to 180° east, for a total of 360°. Chicago, for example, is 87° west of Greenwich, and Los Angeles is 118° west of Greenwich. In the opposite direction are Sydney, Australia, at 151° east of Greenwich, and Hong Kong at 114° east.

Latitude runs east and west, with the equator designated as 0° latitude. Global locations are measured in degrees north or south of the equator, and extend 180° to both the North and South Poles. Los Angeles is 34° north, Chicago is 42° north, Hong Kong is 22° north, and Sydney is 34° south.

A particular location, such as your birthplace, is thus defined by the longitudinal and latitudinal lines that intersect in that place, much like crosshairs.

Longitude corresponds to the Midheaven/IC axis (fourth/tenth-house cusps), and latitude is the Ascendant/Descendant axis (first/seventh-house cusps).

A birth chart is calculated using the birth date, time, and place. The charts of two people born at the same moment but in different time zones, and thus at different longitudes and latitudes, will have planets in the exact same signs, degrees, and minutes. But the angles and house cusps in their charts will have different signs, degrees, and minutes.

Look at the map and overlaid charts illustrated in chart 2. Each chart is calculated for the same time but in the appropriate time zone. The person in this example, if born in Providence, Rhode Island, would have the Midheaven/IC at 17°59' Aquarius/Leo and the Ascendant/Descendant at 13°30' Gemini/Sagittarius. This same person, if born in Los Angeles, California, would have the Midheaven/IC at 29°33' Sagittarius/Gemini and the Ascendant/Descendant at 28°59' Pisces/Virgo.

Using the same principle, you can relocate your birth chart to a different location, thus changing the angles and moving some or all planets to different houses. It's important to understand, however, that, depending upon your birthplace, your Midheaven/IC and Ascendant/Descendant signs will change about three signs at most within the continental United States.

The following table will give you an idea of the signs on the Midheaven based on whether your birth location is in the eastern, central, or western area of the country. All signs on the Midheaven are possible if you're willing to relocate anywhere in the world. (The same is somewhat true of the Ascendant, although it does not change signs as dramatically as does the Midheaven, and is thus more difficult to estimate. A relocated Ascendant might change one or two signs within the continental United States, depending upon your birth location.)

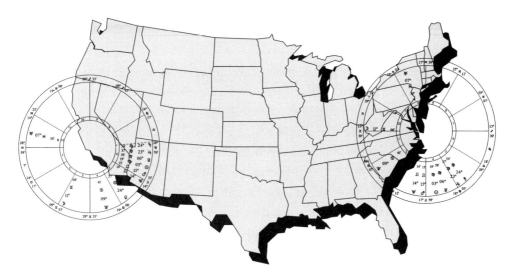

Chart 2
Birth Chart Locations

Midheaven West	*Midheaven Central*	*Midheaven East*
Leo	Virgo	Libra
Virgo	Libra	Scorpio
Libra	Scorpio	Sagittarius
Scorpio	Sagittarius	Capricorn
Sagittarius	Capricorn	Aquarius
Capricorn	Aquarius	Pisces
Aquarius	Pisces	Aries
Pisces	Aries	Taurus
Aries	Taurus	Gemini
Taurus	Gemini	Cancer
Gemini	Cancer	Leo
Cancer	Leo	Virgo

Bill Clinton's chart relocated from Hope, Arkansas, to Washington, D.C. (chart 3), is a good example of how a chart changes when moved east from the birthplace approximately 1,000 miles.

The relocated Midheaven and Ascendant are in the same signs as in his birth chart (Cancer and Libra). The Sun, Moon, Mercury, Jupiter, Saturn, and Uranus are still in their natal houses, but the other four planets—Mars, Neptune, Venus, and Pluto—changed houses. Notice also that in the relocated chart the Moon is sextile the Midheaven, and Jupiter is square the Midheaven. Jupiter also forms a conjunction with the relocated Ascendant, and the Moon makes an inconjunct to it.

The changes in Bill Clinton's chart as relocated to Washington, D.C., are significant in terms of the events that unfolded during his administration, as well as his continuing popularity. In chapter 10, we'll look at the reasons why and explore these charts in more detail.

If you want to calculate a relocated chart without using the CD-ROM, first enter your birth data, including the birth location, and note the time zone. Then, calculate a new chart using your actual birth time (do not adjust for any time zone change in the new location), and enter the new location. If the new location is in a different time zone from that of your birth, manually change the time zone to your birth time zone.

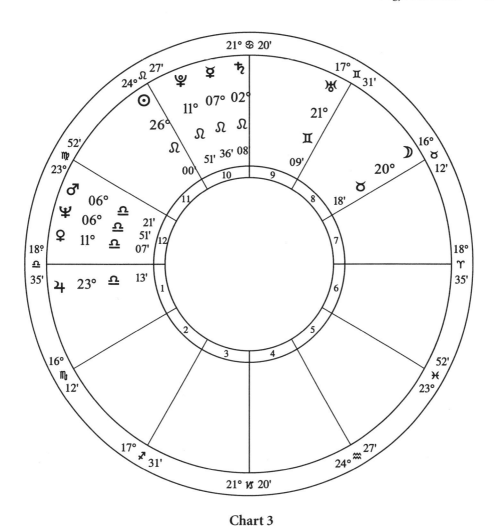

Chart 3
Bill Clinton, Chart Relocated to Washington, D.C.
August 19, 1946 / Washington, D.C. / 8:51 AM CST +6:00
Placidus Houses

2
The Planets

The planets have a starring role in mapping your travels and relocation. Their house positions and aspects to the Midheaven/IC (tenth- and fourth-house cusps) and Ascendant/Descendant (first- and seventh-house cusps) reveal the emphasis, as well as potential events, in locations different from your birthplace. The more familiar you become with the planetary energies, the easier it will be to identify positive prospective locations and those best avoided.

Each planet in your birth chart represents a different drive in your nature. Mercury, for example, represents your need to think and to communicate, and Jupiter symbolizes higher education, religion, travel, and adventure. Thus, by putting certain birth chart planets in higher focus—in particular geographic locations—you can make those drives more prominent and active in your life.

You also might discover hidden talents and strengths you've never before had an opportunity to explore. If, for example, you want to develop your intuition or creative or artistic interests, a prominently placed Neptune could help you achieve that goal. If you want energy and initiative in your life, you could choose a location that highlights your birth chart Mars, the planet of vitality, get-up-and-go, and independent action.

Keep in mind, though, that there's no guarantee the positive qualities of any planet will be in force 100 percent of the time. For example, Mars represents initiative but also accidents; Jupiter signals luck but also tends toward excess; and Neptune signifies inspiration but also confusion. As in all of life, perfection is nonexistent.

It's also important to remember that the planetary aspects in your birth chart are active in all locations. Someone with a natal (birth chart) Venus-Uranus opposition, for example, is prone to tumultuous yet exciting relationships. So, even in a location where Venus positively aspects the Descendant (seventh-house cusp, relationship angle), the opposition will be operative, although with the opportunity to resolve the difficulties represented by the aspect (on-again, off-again relationships; breakups; need for independence) and experience the positive (stimulating and insightful relationships; spontaneity; lasting love at first sight).

The cast of planetary characters is made up of three major groups: the Heavies, the Favorites, and the Middle Children.

The Heavies

The Heavies are Saturn, Neptune, and Pluto. These planets represent very strong, powerful drives in your nature. They are involved with issues that are intense and demanding for most people. Most people would probably prefer to not have any of the Heavies in high focus in their charts and would steer clear of a relocation that placed one of the Heavies in a prominent position. There are, however, times when you might decide you need to accentuate the impulses represented by the Heavies—usually for a limited period of time.

Saturn

Saturn is the planet of reality, responsibility, and reliability. It represents hard work, paying your dues, conventional approaches, and making your way to the top through effort and discipline. Saturn also represents time (and delays), limitation, restriction, rules, and regulations. Most people have more than enough of what Saturn represents in their lives. However, someone who has a mammoth project to accomplish might choose a location that emphasizes Saturn in order to reinforce self-discipline and productive accomplishment. Someone who has lived a "grasshopper life" (flitting from interest to interest; no real focus; few accomplishments) might choose to live for a time in a Saturn region to encourage responsibility and productivity.

Neptune

Neptune is the planet of dreams, illusion, confusion, compassion, deception, drugs, alcohol, imagination, visualization, idealization, mysticism, and otherworldly motifs. Neptune is also a planet of beauty (humanmade as well as nature's wonders). For most people, a placement that highlights Neptune is not a good idea. However, if you are a professional artist, in the world of stage and film, or a healer, you can probably handle very well the drives that Neptune represents.

Pluto

Pluto is the planet of intensity, compulsion, obsession, and seeing things through to the very end. It rules garbage and recycling, therapy, toxic waste, joint resources, and politics. The downside of a Pluto focus can be constant power struggles, particularly over money or sex, or lots of emotional storms. Emotional blackmail, intimidation, manipulation, and covert operations are all possible. You might find things (possessions, jobs, relationships) eliminated from your life that you would have preferred to keep. On the positive side, Pluto represents self-mastery and self-control. A Pluto place would be appropriate for giving up an addiction, such as smoking or drinking, being successful with a diet, or other personal and life transformations that require much concentration, focus, and willpower.

The Middle Children

The Middle Children are Mars, Jupiter, and Uranus. The Middle Children have lots of potential but need to be used with proper care and planning. These planets have an unpredictable side to their nature in that what initially might seem positive can backfire, sooner or later.

Mars

Mars is a key to physical energy and vitality, and represents independence, initiative, courage, and forthright behavior. Mars also symbolizes competition, warfare, self-centeredness, and impulsivity. Moving to an area where Mars is strong in your chart could be very helpful for sports training, strengthening your muscles and physical body, taking charge of your life, breaking loose from entanglements, and focusing on yourself. When Mars principles are overemphasized, however, people can fight and argue a lot, suffer from burnout, anger easily, or become too self-oriented.

Jupiter

If you're familiar with planetary characteristics, you might be surprised that Jupiter is one of the Middle Children instead of one of the Favorites. Jupiter is often portrayed as a cosmic Santa Claus, bringing you all sorts of goodies. That can be true. It is possible, however, to have too much of a good thing. Excesses are not always healthy! Jupiter represents growth, expansion, good times, optimism, luck, opportunity, travel, education, enlightenment, other cultures, exploratory urges, and the quest for the best. People who need a "lift" will often benefit from a Jupiter location. If, however, you're inclined toward rashness, too much faith, or a tendency to move too quickly or without sufficient forethought, putting Jupiter in high focus is probably not a good idea. Also, many people want to expand and enlarge their pocketbooks, but few people want to expand and enlarge their waistlines. Be sensible about where you center that potential for more! The "quest for the best" that Jupiter symbolizes can also lead to excessive idealism, wanting more than is possible, or yearning for an unattainable goal. So, when dealing with Jupiter, examine your standards, your expectations, and what you hope to achieve, and then make sure they are reasonable.

Uranus

Uranus is your "get out of jail free" card. This planet represents revolution, change, innovation, invention, progress, the cutting edge, and everything new and different. Uranus is radical and questions the status quo. If you are feeling confined, hemmed in, trapped, or overwhelmed by a conventional lifestyle, moving to a Uranus-emphasized area could release your inner rebel and ring your personal Liberty Bell. If you are already inclined toward rabble-rousing or upsetting the apple cart, you probably don't need more Uranus in your life!

The Favorites

The Favorites are Venus, Mercury, the Sun, and the Moon. (Astrologers call the Sun and Moon planets for convenience even though the Sun is a star and the Moon is a satellite.) These bodies represent drives that are affirming for most people. In general, putting any of these four in high focus will make it easier for you to tap into the skills they represent.

Venus

Venus is the planet of love, affection, pleasure, indulgence, goods, goodies (including money), and comfort. Few people would object to having more of any of these qualities and items! So, when you're looking for love (relationships), putting Venus in high focus is a good move. Your capacity for partnership is highlighted, and giving and getting affection is likely to flow more easily. Venus is also a planet of beauty (along with Neptune), and thus can be an asset in artistic or creative projects. If you want to relax, pamper yourself, or have a really indulgent vacation, consider a place that emphasizes Venus. One caveat: As with Jupiter, Venus makes it easy to overindulge—and reap the unfortunate consequences (e.g., gaining weight, having a less-than-optimally healthy body). Even Venus can be overdone. Most of the time, however, an emphasis on Venus also emphasizes pleasure, both from the material world and from relationships.

Mercury

Mercury is the planet of communication, particularly verbal, though it can also represent written words. Mercury is a key to the logical, rational mind, and to curiosity and the need to know. Mercury symbolizes flexibility, versatility, multiple talents, a light-hearted style, and the urge to learn. Put Mercury in high focus if you are a student or if you work in the media, communication, or information fields. When you want to juggle multiple projects, a strong Mercury is advisable. One caveat: If you are inclined to be a dilettante, to be scattered, and have too many interests, you probably don't need more Mercury in your life. Generally, however, an emphasis on Mercury in your relocated chart will aid thinking and communication skills.

Sun

The Sun represents your ego and self-esteem. The stronger your Sun is, the better able you are to shine, to lead, to take center stage, to be significant and noteworthy, and to gain attention and applause from the world. The Sun is a key to drama, charisma, and star power. Like Mars, the Sun can accentuate personal vitality. If you want more attention and recognition, moving to a locale that highlights your Sun may help. If you have ambitions to be a mover and shaker, a leader in the world or a particular field, find an arena where your Sun can really shine! One caveat: We have only to look at certain politicians to see the dangers of an excessive ego. Too much Sun can indicate the arrogant prima donna, the person who believes he or she has been granted divine rights. Most of us, however, suffer from low self-esteem rather than excessive pride, so strengthening the Sun is probably a good idea.

Moon

The Moon reflects home, family, domestic matters, feelings, safety, protection, security, food, shelter, clothing, land, real estate, and matters relating to the homeland and the public. If you plan a career in real estate or the restaurant business, a strong Moon could be helpful. If your domestic life is not as developed as you would like, moving to a location that emphasizes the Moon might help you give more priority to home and family matters. The negative side of the Moon is needy, whiny, and dependent—or the "smother mother." So, too much Moon in a horoscope may come across as a demanding child or someone who is too busy looking after what he or she thinks everyone else needs. The individual who is already emotional, reactive, and sensitive is advised against adding emphasis to the Moon. Generally, however, a prominently relocated birth chart Moon will highlight strong emotional connections and family ties.

3
The Angles

In chapter 1, you learned about the chart angles (Ascendant, Descendant, Midheaven, and IC) and how they and geographic locations are defined according to longitude and latitude. To review: The angles are the most personal parts of your chart because they depend totally on your birth time and place. They also represent major life areas: the Ascendant, your individual self-expression and bodily functioning; the Descendant, your relationships (especially marriage and partnerships); the IC, your home, family, and domestic circumstances; and the Midheaven, your status, career, and gift(s) to society.

A rough rule of thumb to use when considering relocation is that 1° of longitude is roughly equivalent to 1° of the sign on your Midheaven/IC axis (for example, 16° Aries to 17° Aries). If you move east, your Midheaven moves to a higher degree. If you move west, your Midheaven moves to a lower degree. For example, a birth chart Midheaven of 16° Scorpio at the birthplace decreases to 9° Scorpio when the relocated chart is calculated for 7° longitude to the west.

The Midheaven changes signs when it is moved far enough to the longitude east or west of the birthplace. Remember, there are 30° in each sign, and twelve signs in the zodiac. The natural order of the signs is Aries, Taurus, Gemini, Cancer, Leo, Virgo, Libra, Scorpio, Sagittarius, Capricorn, Aquarius, Pisces; and, as you also learned in chapter 1, depending upon your birthplace and how far you move, your Midheaven sign will change a maximum of three signs within the continental United States.

The movement of the Ascendant/Descendant is less regular. Generally, moving east to west (or vice versa) will change your horoscope more than moving north to south (or vice versa).

The easiest way to emphasize a particular planet is to align it by planetary aspect with one of the angles of your chart. If, for example, you want to pursue a career in writing, sales, or media work, moving to a location that aligns Mercury (communication) with your Midheaven (career) would be a good idea.

The most intense form of alignment would be to move to a place where a particular planet makes a conjunction aspect (occupying the same degree of the zodiac) to one of your angles. In some cases, this makes the energy more concentrated than is considered desirable, so a viable alternative would be to have the planet in harmonious aspect (sextile or trine) to one of the angles. Harmonious aspects indicate the likelihood of a smooth, easy flow, and talents and abilities are usually readily accessed. Challenging aspects (square, quincunx, opposition) are generally to be avoided because they can indicate competition, inner conflict, and outward clashes.

Occasionally an individual will choose, consciously or subconsciously, to move to an area where a planet makes a challenging aspect to an angle as an aid in learning a major life lesson. Usually, however, it's wise to avoid challenging aspects to angles.

Part of the reason a planet in conjunction aspect to an angle is so intense is because any planet that is conjunct one angle is opposite the other (Ascendant/Descendant, and Midheaven/IC). So, the potential for strength and focus has a flip side—the potential for clashes and challenges. For this reason, and because harmony aspects are reciprocal (if a planet is trine one angle, it is sextile the other angle of that axis), many people prefer to select locations where specific planets make harmonious aspects with the angles.

Important Note on Orbs: The same planetary orbs are used in natal (birth) and relocated charts (see chapter 1). However, a maximum orb of *4° or less* to a relocated angle is highly recommended before seriously considering a move to a specific area.

Dr. Zipporah Dobyns

Maritha Pottenger's mother, Zipporah (Zip) Dobyns, was born in Chicago, and her natal Midheaven is 1°57' Aquarius, with 24°25' Taurus on the Ascendant (chart 4).

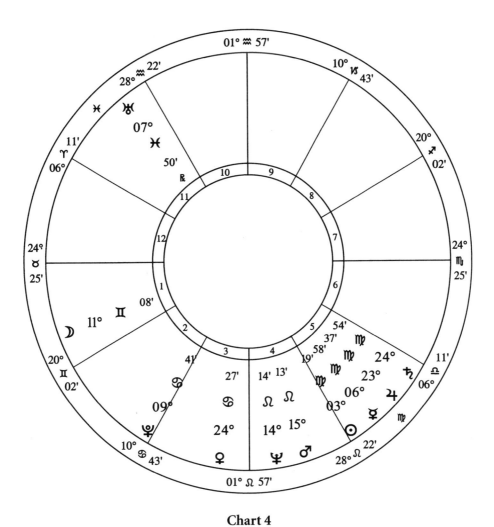

Chart 4
Zipporah Dobyns, Birth Chart
August 26, 1921 / Chicago, IL / 9:48 PM CST +6:00
Placidus Houses

When the chart is relocated to Birmingham, Alabama (chart 5), which is about the same longitude as Chicago but about 8° south in latitude, note that the Midheaven changes less than 1°, while the Ascendant moves almost 5°. However, when the birth chart is relocated to Seattle, Washington (chart 6), which is 122° west longitude, or approximately 35° west of Chicago, the chart changes dramatically; the Midheaven is 29°33' Sagittarius, and the Ascendant is 28°59' Pisces.

Chicago's latitude is 41°51' north. Locations east and west of Chicago, along the same approximate latitude, are Providence, Rhode Island; Cedar Rapids, Iowa; and Medicine Bow, Wyoming. Providence is about 16° east of Chicago, and the relocated Midheaven is about 16° higher than the birthplace Midheaven, or 17°59' Aquarius. Cedar Rapids is about 4° west of Chicago, and the relocated Midheaven there is almost 4° lower than the birthplace Midheaven, or 28°06' Capricorn. Moving farther west, Medicine Bow is about 19° west of Chicago; there, the relocated Midheaven is about 18° lower than the birthplace Midheaven, or 14°24' Capricorn.

Note that by relocating the birth chart to Seattle (as well as other locations in the far western United States), there is a huge stellium (three or more planets in conjunction) in the sixth house. If an individual were extremely wrapped up in his or her work or very involved with nutrition or health and healing activities, that might be okay. Most people, however, would go into overload with such an emphasis and likely be overworked or constantly involved in health issues. Zip settled on the West Coast and was a workaholic for the last thirty-five years of her life, using the relocated sixth-house Sun trine the Midheaven to build her career and gain recognition as an astrologer.

In Providence (chart 7), however, the focus would have been on family and nurturing or maternal motifs since the relocated chart has the Moon conjunct the Ascendant, Mars and Neptune conjunct the IC, and the Sun and Mercury in the fourth house.

Medicine Bow (chart 8) offers the possibility of a bit more fun because the natal Taurus (practical earth sign) Ascendant, when relocated, moves to Aries (extroverted fire sign). Jupiter and Saturn in Virgo move into the sixth house, where they are more "at home" because Virgo is the sixth sign in the zodiac and, therefore, the sign universally associated with the sixth house. Mars and Neptune, which are in the natal fourth house, move into the fifth house of children, creativity, recreation, romance, and entertainment in the relocated chart.

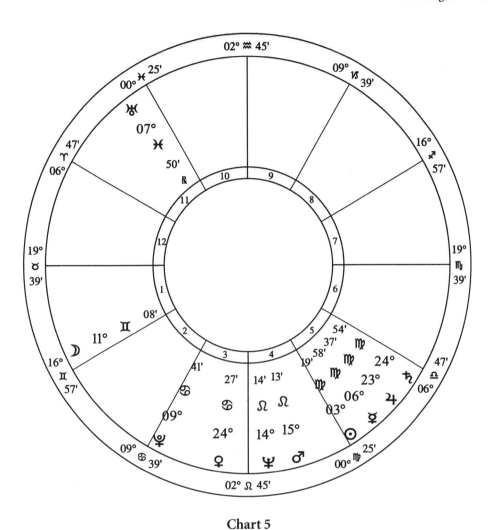

Chart 5
Zipporah Dobyns, Chart Relocated to Birmingham, AL
August 26, 1921 / Birmingham, AL / 9:48 PM CST +6:00
Placidus Houses

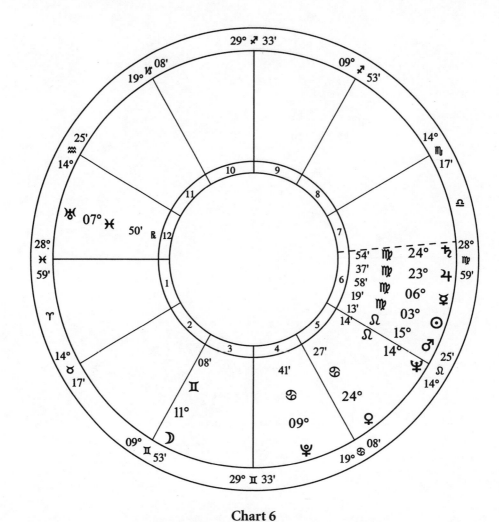

Chart 6
Zipporah Dobyns, Chart Relocated to Seattle, WA
August 26, 1921 / Seattle, WA / 9:48 PM CST +6:00
Placidus Houses

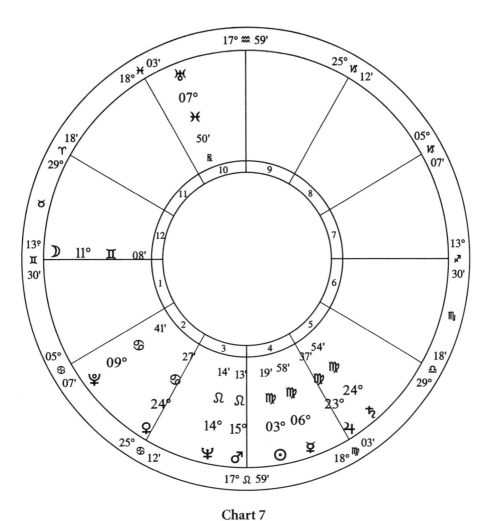

Chart 7
Zipporah Dobyns, Chart Relocated to Providence, RI
August 26, 1921 / Providence, RI / 9:48 PM CST +6:00
Placidus Houses

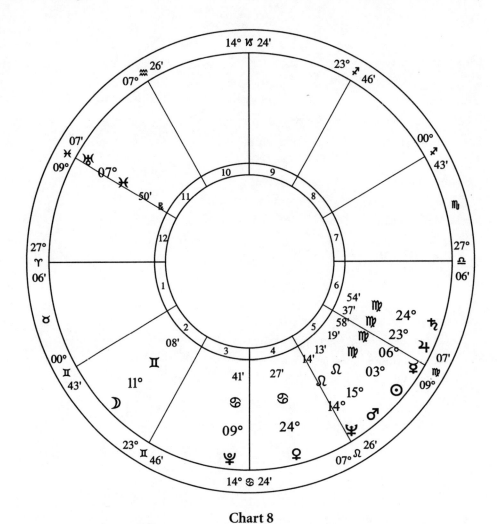

Chart 8
Zipporah Dobyns, Chart Relocated to Medicine Bow, WY
August 26, 1921 / Medicine Bow, WY / 9:48 PM CST +6:00
Placidus Houses

Relocation Results

A man who relocated in order to care for his ill mother has natal Neptune (compassion and rescuing instincts) sextile his Ascendant in that locale. (His natal Neptune also is conjunct the Moon, the planet that symbolizes mother or mother figure.) His mother passed away three years after he moved to her location, where his relocated chart also features Pluto (life-and-death matters, elimination, letting go) conjunct his Ascendant, and the Moon (mother) quincunx (separation) his Midheaven.

Another man who moved for work reasons has Mercury trine the Midheaven (from the second house of money and material possessions) in the new location. He prospered financially there, where he used Mercury's intellectual emphasis, as well as other traits represented by this planet—"eye-mind-hand" coordination and mechanical/repair skills—in his job.

For twenty years, Maritha Pottenger and her mother, Zip Dobyns, taught Astrology Intensives at the Feathered Pipe Ranch outside Helena, Montana. The eight- to fourteen-day programs focused on astrology and psychotherapy techniques and were emotionally intense. People shared a great deal (all day and well into every evening) with each other and often felt almost like a family at the end of a session. Maritha's chart relocated to Helena has Uranus (astrology) conjunct the Ascendant, while Zip's relocated chart has Pluto (depth psychotherapy) conjunct the IC.

A man who decided to retire in a different location lives where Mercury is conjunct the Ascendant, and spends much of his time reading, an appropriate Mercury-ruled activity. He also stays busy doing minor repairs, carpentry, and similar projects that utilize the dexterity and "skillful hands" potential of Mercury.

A woman who moved to a location where Mars squares the Ascendant and Venus squares the Midheaven/IC axis has found her parental responsibilities to be a handicap in terms of developing romantic partnerships. Issues concerning ideals, beliefs, and values have been central in her challenges with men, and she also is more outspoken and direct with authority figures and more physically active in the new location.

Another person had his first serious relationship and love affair in a location where Venus is square the Midheaven. The relationship was with an older woman, symbolized by Venus (relationships) in Capricorn (older people).

Sometimes astrology is amazingly literal. Maritha met her life partner in Los Angeles, a location that puts Uranus (astrology = Maritha) conjunct his Descendant (relationships). The relocated chart also puts his Descendant in the same sign and degree as Maritha's Ascendant (self).

Kris Brandt Riske fulfilled her desire to become a writer when she moved to Arizona. There, her relocated chart has Mercury and Saturn trine the Midheaven (career), and three planets in the sixth house of work. Mercury and Saturn are also, of course, trine in her natal chart, and the relocation helped her use the birth chart potential of this writer's aspect.

Now that you're aware of some of the possibilities indicated by relocation, look at your birth chart and list the aspects to the Midheaven, IC, Ascendant, and Descendant. Next, using the CD-ROM to create the charts, do the same for other locations you've lived in or visited, especially those where major events occurred or that you particularly liked or disliked. Then read the appropriate interpretations in chapter 4.

4
Planets Aspecting the Angles

Planets aspecting the chart angles (Ascendant, Descendant, Midheaven, IC) reveal much about the experiences, interests, and events that can occur in a particular location. This also can help you make the most of your birth chart potential by emphasizing a particular talent or skill.

It's important to remember, however, that if your birth chart shows little potential for becoming a concert pianist or an engineer, or achieving Hollywood stardom, for example, relocation won't change that fact. So, be honest with yourself, and first identify your strengths, weaknesses, abilities, interests, and realistic life mission. That way you increase the odds of maximizing your success potential through relocation.

Also keep in mind that a difficult aspect (square, opposition, and some conjunctions) in your birth chart becomes no less so in a relocated one. However, through awareness and by having such an aspect in harmony with the angles at a new location, you have the opportunity to explore and potentially resolve the life issues that the birth chart aspect represents.

If you haven't yet done so, calculate your birth chart using the CD-ROM included with this book, and make a list of the aspects (lines in the center of the chart). Then read about the planets in your chart that aspect the angles at your birthplace. (If you did not spend a significant number of childhood and teenage years at your birthplace, calculate your chart for the location, or locations, where you lived the longest.) This is a good starting point because you'll quickly see how planets aspecting the angles play out in real life.

Then move on to calculate relocated charts (using the CD-ROM) for areas that attract you and those you're considering moving to. Finally, look for locations that add emphasis to your life goals and desires by placing certain planets in aspect to the angles. To make it easy, calculate relocated charts for cities on the East and West Coasts and central United States so you can see how the angles change at various locations.

Sun

Sun Conjunction Midheaven-Opposition IC

If you're very career-directed, this placement accentuates that trait, and there is a good possibility for increased professional recognition or renown. But that might be at the expense of a less domestic focus, and family members who feel your attention is too much on the world of work. You also might look for ways to generate more excitement, fun, or creativity in your job, or work in fields that accent recreation, entertainment, drama, or leadership. A strong sense of personal pride in your accomplishments and status is possible, but if ego issues with authority figures (including bosses) are a problem, you could run into difficulties at this location. Nevertheless, the potential exists for reaching great heights in your vocation, and this placement is excellent for speculation, creative endeavors, and jobs in the entertainment industry and working with children.

Sun Conjunction IC-Opposition Midheaven

You might want to avoid this placement if you feel under-appreciated or rarely receive adequate recognition in your career. Although the possibility of happy exchanges on the home front is increased, there is also the potential to feel that others get the professional attention and applause you deserve. Love and warmth are highlighted, and the desire for a home and family is usually overly emphasized. You could receive more admiration or attention for domestic skills or activities within the nest, and you might want to turn your home into a showplace.

Sun Conjunction Ascendant-Opposition Descendant

If you're already self-confident and able to put yourself first, this might not be an ideal placement because this combination is less inclined to compromise in relationships and you could adopt a "divine right" attitude. Personal magnetism and charisma could increase, however, and you probably are willing to take more risks (might gamble). In this location your inner child is accented, with a high level of enthusiasm and creativity, and you might feel more vital and alive, an active participant in the world.

Sun Conjunction Descendant-Opposition Ascendant

If you already tend to "give away" some of your own charisma to other people, this is a location you might want to avoid. It would be easier for you to see others as magnetic, dynamic, and larger than life, but you might often hide your own light under a bushel. Excitement and thrills are sought in relationships, and you can attract people who are generous, passionate, dynamic, and full of praise. You also could enjoy a mutual admiration society with partners.

Sun Sextile/Trine Midheaven/IC

In this location you could effectively use creative skills to further your vocational aims, and personal charisma and persuasive abilities could be professional assets. You might do more teaching or delve into other vocational pursuits that put you center stage. Authority figures and loved ones can be the source of an encouraging word or helpful hand, and your pride and urge for recognition will contribute to your achievements. Promotional skills can help you do well in your field, and you can achieve more professional notice (perhaps even fame) in this locale.

Sun Sextile/Trine Ascendant/Descendant

You might find it easier to express your creative side in this location, and your leadership instincts could pour out more smoothly, along with charisma and enthusiasm. Romantic urges may increase, and the desire to love and be loved could be a stronger part of your personal expression. You also could be more involved with play, entertainment, or exciting or onstage activities. Praise, appreciation, and admiration flow more easily and naturally in relationships.

Sun Square/Quincunx Ascendant/Descendant

Issues of personal self-esteem could be in focus here, and you might struggle with an overly inflated ego (arrogance, a prima donna attitude) or too little self-esteem. Perhaps you overdo the desire for play and recreation, or don't know how to celebrate life and love. You might feel that others inhibit your capacity for creativity and joy, or that you must deal with people who try to upstage you. Your challenge is to find healthy ways to be center stage and to take reasonable risks.

Sun Square/Quincunx Midheaven/IC

You could face challenges from authority figures regarding your ambitions or status, and loved ones, including children, could compete with your vocational goals (in terms of time and energy). The balancing act between love and work may be difficult, and pride and pragmatism may be at odds as well. Creative abilities are accented but may not always be optimally expressed. Your challenge is to find a way to be special and to shine while also being sensible, responsible, and productive.

Moon

Moon Conjunction Midheaven-Opposition IC

You might become more involved with women, the land, real estate, the public, commodities (food, shelter, clothing, etc.), emotions, the sea, or protective, caretaking pursuits in your professional life. You also could nurture the careers of others, acting as a mentor for younger people. Security is a major priority in this location, and you might seek safety through gaining power or status, or by being an authority figure. Parental issues (your own parents and your role as a parent) move into higher focus, and you will be more aware of the need to balance domestic duties and desires with contributions to the world at large.

Moon Conjunction IC-Opposition Midheaven

Family focus is strengthened and deepened in this location, and you might spend more time in the nest, with family members, or doing things that relate to the home, land, real estate, food, shelter, clothing, or basic emotional safety. Old feelings about a mother figure(s) could be triggered, with the chance to work through issues. Protection is a major drive, whether you strive to protect yourself, look after others, or both. Depending upon other factors in the chart and your current life circumstances, this placement can accentuate maternal instincts (even to the extreme of the "smother mother" tendency) or highlight feelings of dependency and vulnerability. Establishing an emotionally and physically secure home base is essential.

Moon Conjunction Ascendant-Opposition Descendant

Your body might be more sensitive to the environment here, and food issues can move into higher focus. Moodiness, security needs, receptivity, and vulnerability might become more emphasized. Emotional attachments move up on the priority list, and you might be more active with family members or more involved with domestic matters. Although you could feel torn between looking after yourself and protecting others, this is a good placement for learning to more fully nurture yourself.

Moon Conjunction Descendant-Opposition Ascendant

Relationships are likely to emphasize emotional security, and mutual nurturing can occur, with you and others being supportive of each other. Or, what should be a partnership could operate more like a mother-child relationship, with you playing the role of the protective parent or the needy, dependent kid. Warmth and family feelings are highlighted. Emotional connections are a greater priority in this location.

Moon Sextile/Trine Midheaven/IC

Family members may assist you professionally, domestic circumstances could prove to be more supportive of your vocational aspirations, and women, emotions, or the public could contribute to your status and success. You're likely to have a good balance between compassion and competence, between nurturing and the bottom line, between gentle caring and pragmatic capability. Security needs are reinforced. You can move easily between the private and public worlds.

Moon Sextile/Trine Ascendant/Descendant

This area is apt to support your domestic instincts and desire for security, emotional attachments, and nesting behavior. Emotional matters are highlighted. You may increase the caretaking you do of others, or feel greater dependency and the need for the assistance of those you love. Your personal actions tend to flow naturally into activities that involve home, children, family, food, or building a secure foundation. It will probably be easier for you to balance your personal needs with the needs of others in this location.

Moon Square/Quincunx Midheaven/IC

You may feel that your domestic needs are at odds with your professional ambitions in this location, where challenges could arise regarding women, the public, emotional matters, parental responsibilities, or the quest for security. Pragmatism could vie with sensitivity and compassion. You may feel torn between looking after family members versus pursuing a career or making a contribution to the wider world. Your task is to find a comfortable blend of caring and competence, of warmth and the bottom line, to do your duty both in terms of the nest and loved ones as well as vocational demands.

Moon Square/Quincunx Ascendant/Descendant

In this location conflicts could arise between you and women, children, your mother, or nurturing figures and family members. You may feel torn between meeting your personal needs and attending to the needs of others. Questions of support, especially on an emotional level, could arise. Food issues might intensify. You may feel your security is threatened through relationships or through what you feel you have to do here. Your challenge is to find a happy medium between dependency and independence, initiative and receptivity.

Mercury

Mercury Conjunction Midheaven-Opposition IC

You could bring more learning, thinking, communicating, logic, listening, talking, writing, dexterity, variety, commerce, media contacts, paperwork, or versatility into your career in this location. Your mind is apt to be more focused on issues of realism, responsibility, and reliability, and thus you might be more susceptible to your inner critic. But this also is an opportunity to broaden your perceptions of reality, to see more options. You can be very productive with your mind and may work at gathering or disseminating information. Facts and figures are more accessible to you. Dual careers (two at once) are one of your options here.

Mercury Conjunction IC-Opposition Midheaven

This locale highlights restlessness in the domestic realm. You may feel the urge to move more often, or to change things around within the nest. Boredom is closer to the surface; you seek variety and mental stimulation. This can lead to many short trips, discussions with the neighbors, people visiting, or doing lots of writing or teaching within or from your home. You might discover that your memory is better here, and your thoughts and feelings are likely to blend, one influencing the other. You also often provide reassurance to others through your words and ideas.

Mercury Conjunction Ascendant-Opposition Descendant

Your communication skills could increase exponentially. (Of course, you might also talk incessantly in this locale!) Flexibility, learning, intellectual curiosity and restlessness, and the need to know are all highlighted. You may talk or read more, or be more active in using your hands with increased dexterity. Your objectivity and observational skills could be sharpened, and you might discover you're wittier (quicker on the uptake, with quips, comebacks, and rapid repartee) and that your thinking processes have speeded up.

Mercury Conjunction Descendant-Opposition Ascendant

Communication is emphasized in relationships, and a meeting of the minds is likely. Too much talking (or too much listening) is possible; find a happy medium. A partner might be more flighty, scattered, or inclined to go off in many different directions. If you tend to undervalue your own intellectual abilities, this is a placement to avoid because you could view others as brighter and more articulate than yourself. Humor is likely to be featured in interpersonal exchanges, and contacts with others could help you develop more objectivity, logic, or lightheartedness.

Mercury Sextile/Trine Midheaven/IC

Your communication skills, flexibility, media contacts, commercial instincts, sociability, or multiple talents could all be professional assets. Your career might be advanced by relatives, other people you know, dexterity, writing, speaking, or intellect. You can deal well with paperwork, and excel at gathering information and passing it on to others in an effective manner. Objectivity, logic, and good problem-solving abilities are highlighted. Your perceptions are an important part of your contribution to society.

Mercury Sextile/Trine Ascendant/Descendant

You may find it easier to think, talk, write, reason, or deal with intellectual matters in this location, where objectivity and logic are strong assets. Your awareness could increase, along with dexterity, adaptability, and eye-mind-hand coordination. Listening skills are highlighted, as is the ability to communicate effectively. You could be noted for your public-speaking, writing, or other communication skills that emphasize one-on-one connections.

Mercury Square/Quincunx Midheaven/IC

Thoughts and communication could trigger a clash with authority figures or the powers that be, or perhaps a lighthearted attitude competes with a sober, serious approach. Power struggles with relatives are possible. Too much or too little talking could be a professional issue, and challenges could arise over paperwork, adaptability, the media, or commercial interactions. Your logic and reasoning may differ from conventional wisdom. Professional duties may compete with your social life. Much mental restlessness or activity is possible in your vocational life, where your challenge is to use curiosity and intellectual skills to advance your status.

Mercury Square/Quincunx Ascendant/Descendant

Communication blockages or barriers could develop here, where perhaps you feel your thinking is less clear or objective. There could be an imbalance in your relationships between listening and talking, and knowing when to think (or discuss) and when to act might be difficult. Sarcasm, arguments, or sharp verbal exchanges could increase, and multiple interests could pull you in too many directions. Your challenge is to accent flexibility and sharp thinking in ways that enhance your personal freedom and self-expression.

Venus

Venus Conjunction Midheaven-Opposition IC

You might come to enjoy your career more in this location, or your profession could provide more income, gratification, sensual satisfaction, or involvement with beauty.

Your grace, charm, and pleasant manner could be professional assets, and you might be more inclined to seek an easy job or to look for opportunities to share with other people. Teamwork is appealing. You might meet a spouse through your work or feel like you're married to your career. Comfort, stability, security, and predictability go up on the priority list, particularly regarding your vocation. You're likely to become more practical about financial matters, and reality is highlighted.

Venus Conjunction IC-Opposition Midheaven

This location accents the connection between home and pleasure, and thus you might feel gratified by spending time with loved ones, being in the nest, or taking care of domestic tasks. You could become more fond of cooking (or eating) or enjoy decorating your home. A tactile orientation is highlighted; you are drawn toward what feels good. You also might have a stronger desire to collect things, and could make money through land, real estate, or a home-based business, but could spend extravagantly on anything related to family and your domicile. Love and affection may be more evident with kin, and you might be drawn to genealogy, patriotic activities, history, or other paths to exploring your roots and remembering the past. Sensual satisfaction is likely to increase.

Venus Conjunction Ascendant-Opposition Descendant

Your personal attractiveness could increase in this area as a result of a more charming, graceful manner, and you could become more physically appealing by taking steps to enhance your appearance. You might learn to like yourself better and become more comfortable "in your own skin." A desire for comfort and sensual pleasures could increase. (If indulgence is overdone, weight or health issues are possible.) You could become actively involved in the pursuit of money, possessions, or stability and comfort. Feeling good is a priority. Relationships might become more important because in this location, self-definition comes partially through comparisons with others. You also might become more artistic or involved with issues of justice, equality, and fair play, and a partner could be more willing to assist you. Teamwork can flow more smoothly.

Venus Conjunction Descendant-Opposition Ascendant

Relationships are doubly emphasized. The drive for partnership is likely to be stronger in this location, and sharing and teamwork are priorities. But you or your partner may tend to "keep score" out of a desire to have things fair and equitably divided. Aesthetic abilities could be accentuated, or you or the people you attract could put too much emphasis on appearances and looking good. Gratification is tied to the interpersonal world; you find pleasure in people. You may also attract individuals who are comfort-oriented, stable, and sensual, or for whom financial security is important. The tendency is to expect a smooth, easy flow in the interpersonal realm.

Venus Sextile/Trine Midheaven/IC

Your career and/or status could be enhanced thanks to women, love, partners, sensuality, financial skills, personal grace and charm, beauty, or aesthetic talents. You are likely to be relaxed and comfortable in your pursuit of status and making your contribution to society. Your preference here is for what is stable and familiar, and you might find it easier to generate money and resources. Authorities may be more supportive of your quest for gratification, and your family activities could be more pleasurable.

Venus Sextile/Trine Ascendant/Descendant

You find it natural to take it easy in this location, and seek comfort and pleasure. You expect life to be smoother. Aesthetic abilities and talents can be strengthened, and you could increase your earning power or what you own and enjoy. (Hedonism and laziness are also quite possible.) Kindness, a sweet manner, and affectionate exchanges come more easily. Love is in the air. You are eager to share with others. Your charm quotient rises.

Venus Square/Quincunx Midheaven/IC

Love and work may compete in this locale, and you might feel that pursuing your ambitions keeps you from a partner or inhibits your romantic life. Or, you might feel a partner is a handicap to your career. Duty could vie with pleasure if you feel torn between keeping your nose to the grindstone and relaxing and indulging (particularly sensually and in love relationships). Vocational challenges may be triggered by women, financial matters, or an excessive desire for comfort. Finding a way to combine ease and effort, power and peer relationships, and responsibilities and indulgences will allow you to have the best of both worlds.

Venus Square/Quincunx Ascendant/Descendant

Clashes in relationships are possible. Separations can occur, and widely disparate viewpoints can be an issue in this location. Money is a potential bone of contention. You and those around you may be living a balancing act between assertion and accommodation (and could go to extremes before finding a happy medium). Issues concerning sensuality, physical pleasures, and possessions are apt to arise. Too much or too little indulgence is possible. Who owns what and who has which rights in terms of gratification are likely topics of interest. By mastering the art of appropriate compromise, you can bring more satisfaction to yourself and those you love.

Mars

Mars Conjunction Midheaven-Opposition IC

You might become an entrepreneur in this location, ready to work for yourself and on your own terms. But you also could end up confronting authority figures and might challenge the status quo or fight back against rules or potential limitations. Your initiative and pioneering spirit are likely vocational assets, but anger, irritability, impatience, and boredom ("I do things once and then move on") are potential dangers. You might work more with men, the outdoors, metal tools or weapons, or in any setting in which you are on your own. Here, you can put much energy into achievement, and instinctively rise to meet challenges. You feel most powerful when tangible results are achieved, and your task is to find a way to assert yourself strongly and forcefully within the limits of what is possible in the material world.

Mars Conjunction IC-Opposition Midheaven

This placement suggests lots of action and activity in and around the home, and you may have trouble staying put in this locale. You might add on to your house, rearrange the furniture often, or fill your domestic environment with physically active or independent people. Anger or irritation could be more of an issue regarding domestic duties and household matters, and you're likely to be more centered on getting what you want from family members. A nurturing motif is present, but only on your own terms. You could revisit old issues related to a parent, such as assertion, being yourself, and owning your personal power.

Mars Conjunction Ascendant-Opposition Descendant

You might find it easier to be yourself in this locale, where assertive instincts, independence, a pioneering spirit, and initiative are accented. The drive for immediate gratification could be more compelling, and your energy level might rise. Competitive instincts could also increase, along with irritability and impulsive actions. Owning your personal power should be easier here, and you are probably willing to be the first to break new ground.

Mars Conjunction Descendant-Opposition Ascendant

Relationships may feature more sexual (and other) excitement, energy, and activity, and you could gravitate toward partners who are rash, self-centered, competitive, independent, and eager to go their own way. You might seek partners who encourage you to do your own thing. Anger (and, in extreme cases, violence) could be an issue in your relationships. The challenge is to be true to yourself and your own needs while sharing the world with another person.

Mars Sextile/Trine Midheaven/IC

Your ambitions are on the rise, and you are likely to be active and assertive in pursuit of status and vocational achievements. You put much energy and much of yourself into your work, and may find it easier to get along with authority figures in this location, where men might aid your vocational aspirations. Your pioneering spirit, independence, initiative, courage, and integrity are apt to be assets in your professional life. This placement suggests a good balance between caution and confidence. Your natural instincts are to seek power, authority, and achievements. You will want to do something worthwhile in the wider world.

Mars Sextile/Trine Ascendant/Descendant

Desire (sexual and otherwise) is highlighted, as are your personal will and preferences. This placement is excellent for energy, independence, and getting what you want; however, if those qualities are overemphasized, anger or impulsive actions could be a problem. You might react too quickly, and doing your own thing is high on the priority list. Courage is marked, and expressing yourself is vital. You might find it easier to strengthen your muscles and physical body, and you could become more assertive.

Mars Square/Quincunx Midheaven/IC

Conflicts with authority figures (including parents and bosses) are a real danger in this location. You could be more prone to argue with the people in charge, and your feisty side is easily triggered by people who run the show, because anger and impatience are nearer to the surface. You also could end up fighting with your own conscience, torn between doing what you want to do and doing what you feel you should do. Your challenge is to find a way to get what you want within the rules of the "game" (what is possible in the real, workaday world). If you channel your initiative and energy constructively, you can accomplish quite a lot.

Mars Square/Quincunx Ascendant/Descendant

You may experiment with different forms of self-expression in this locale, or feel pulled between different sides of yourself. Issues could arise around anger—what is appropriate, how much to vent, how to deal with irritability, etc. Fights or competition could develop, and you're likely to feel "stirred up" in this area. In extreme cases, violence (from you or toward you) could be a problem. If you are already susceptible to giving personal power to other people, this is not an advisable placement. Interactions with males may be more challenging. Your task here is to develop a healthy sense of your own personal power—the ability to be independent and active without running roughshod over the rights of others, and without allowing them to take advantage of you. Sports and physically active pursuits are accentuated.

Jupiter

Jupiter Conjunction Midheaven-Opposition IC

Your career in this locale could involve more travel, education, enlightenment, law, beliefs, other cultures, or anything that expands your horizons physically, mentally, or spiritually. You may enlarge your professional capacities, and greater optimism and faith in your area of expertise is possible. Luck or opportunity may come through mentors or Establishment figures, and you have the potential to optimally blend confidence and caution, expansion and contraction. You are likely to place a high value on responsibility, status, and achievement here, where the quest for the best is firmly linked to your ambitions and contributions to the world.

Jupiter Conjunction IC-Opposition Midheaven

You may want a larger, grander home in this location. Or, perhaps you will be drawn to a home in the woods where you can appreciate nature, or one with lots of land. You may fill your home with more books, and welcome philosophical discussions, spiritual activities, or people from other lands or those interested in the pursuit of higher truth. You might travel more or consider a home in another country. This placement accentuates a "quest for the best" where family members are concerned. On the positive side, you can recognize and reinforce the highest potentials in your loved ones. The downside is that you may expect more than is humanly possible from yourself and/or other family members. More commonly, you fill your nest with lots of joy, celebration, and good times.

Jupiter Conjunction Ascendant-Opposition Descendant

Your confidence and optimism are on the upswing, and you take advantage of more opportunities because you are primed to notice them. Lady Luck is riding on your shoulders. You also could go overboard in terms of faith and engage in rash or reckless behavior, rushing in "where angels fear to tread." Excessive behavior is easier to indulge in here, so you might take anything to an extreme by doing too much. Philosophical matters could become more of a personal priority, and honesty and forthright expression are high on your list.

Jupiter Conjunction Descendant-Opposition Ascendant

You may attract people who are involved in philosophy, religion, education, enlightenment, travel, or anything that involves higher truth or far horizons. You are likely to share a sense of humor with others and may encourage optimism in them. If the idealism of this combination is overdone, unreasonable expectations are possible. Either you or your partner may be expecting a perfect, "best of the best" experience rather than a relationship where two fallible human beings are learning together.

Jupiter Sextile/Trine Midheaven/IC

You might find that your values and beliefs are congruent with those of authority figures, and your optimism, intellectual abilities, willingness to risk for greater gain, or adventurous spirit could be vocational assets. You may improve your status because you believe in and pursue the best in life, and could achieve more power and mastery through philosophical perspectives, a gregarious style, honesty, or an attitude of open-ness and exploration. Travel, education, metaphysics, or other questing activities could become an important part of your gift to the world. Luck and opportunity are more readily available to you. You grasp chances for advancement because you expect to spot them.

Jupiter Sextile/Trine Ascendant/Descendant

You could become more involved with travel, education, philosophy, enlightenment, or seeking higher truth in this locale. Your beliefs and values become stronger and more central to your sense of self in this location, where self-confidence and optimism could increase. If overdone, however, these motifs could lead to foolhardy behavior, self-right-eous attitudes, or a tendency to be excessive and exaggerate. Generally, life feels more upbeat; you see endless, exciting possibilities and eagerly pursue opportunities.

Jupiter Square/Quincunx Midheaven/IC

Moral or ethical conflicts and clashes could arise in this locale, particularly with author-ity figures or involving your career or family members. Questions of right and wrong and differing beliefs systems will have to be sorted out. Expectations could be much too high (and unreachable), whether applied by you to others or by others to you, both in regard to professional duties and the domestic arena. Optimism may vie with pes-simism, with extremes on both sides. Your challenge is to know when to expand and when to consolidate your gains; when to reach out confidently and trust that things will work out; and when to move slowly and cautiously. Your visionary side can be helpful if you keep a healthy dose of realism present as well.

Jupiter Square/Quincunx Ascendant/Descendant

In this location you could sometimes act against your better judgment. Your beliefs, val-ues, philosophies, and understanding of higher truths are likely to be called into ques-tion, and you may modify your belief system. You might have to deal with excessive ide-alism—unreasonably high expectations that can lead to frustration. Issues of faith and confidence are in focus. Either extreme—too much trust, with rash, excessive behavior, or too little trust, with a fear to try new things—is unadvisable. This is a location in which you can explore other concepts, build a healthy confidence level and spiritual connection, and make the most of opportunities to expand your possibilities in life.

Saturn

Saturn Conjunction Midheaven-Opposition IC

You're likely to be more aware of the limits of the world and the rules of the game in this locale, and could be more responsible, realistic, hard-working, and competent. You may deal more with established, conventional channels and people, and learning through doing (apprenticeship) is probable. You may ground your expertise and own more of your own power, or feel frustrated and blocked by negative, dominating authority figures (including bosses). Parental motifs and issues could be revisited. Your challenge is to be effective within the limits of what is possible in the material world, neither fighting reality nor giving up too soon. Dedication and thoroughness could increase. You are willing to put much effort into generating measurable results and having a tangible impact on the world.

Saturn Conjunction IC-Opposition Midheaven

You could end up with lots of responsibilities in this region, particularly regarding family members, and may end up carrying too much of the load at home. Facing facts about loved ones is not always pleasant, but is likely to occur here. Old, unresolved feelings about your parents are likely to be triggered so you can work through them. Questions of duty, safety, and who supports whom are apt to emerge. On the down side, you could feel that others are emotionally withholding, constrictive, restrictive, and demanding. On the positive side, you could establish a successful home-based business or do many productive tasks within your home.

Saturn Conjunction Ascendant-Opposition Descendant

In this location you could be more hard-working, ambitious, responsible, reliable, and productive. You might really get your career in gear! Realism is apt to rise. You also will be more aware of limits, restrictions, barriers, and blockages. Challenges with authority figures or health issues (often having to do with constriction or the consequences of unwise lifestyle choices) are possible. Your personal will comes face to face with cosmic laws and the rules and regulations of society. You may push too hard (and hit the stone wall of reality), or you might give up too soon (by assuming you will be frustrated and blocked). Your challenge is to energetically achieve as much as you can within the practical limits of the material world.

Saturn Conjunction Descendant-Opposition Ascendant

You may feel that relationships are a desert in this locale—blocked, frustrated, and limiting. Or, you may experience other people as domineering, controlling, and demanding. On the positive side, you could get involved with individuals who are hard-working, responsible, competent, and eager to make their mark in the world. This placement is good for working partnerships and practical attitudes about sharing. You are willing to put effort into building a healthy exchange with others.

Saturn Sextile/Trine Midheaven/IC

Your reliability, realism, and responsible attitude will be vocational assets in this location. Pragmatism serves you well. You can work your way to the top in terms of career and status because you put forth much effort and are quite willing to pay your dues. Authority figures (including parents) may provide you with aid and assistance. Your ability to determine what needs to be done, and what's possible and impossible, will be valuable in terms of success. You know when to consolidate your gains. Productive and capable, you have natural executive instincts. Your sense of timing is likely to be good. You function well in conventional settings, and can achieve success working within the rules.

Saturn Sextile/Trine Ascendant/Descendant

In this location you could put more of yourself into your career, and could become more focused, realistic, pragmatic, and achievement-oriented. You may learn to handle relationships with authority figures in a healthy, constructive fashion, and can achieve a good balance between personal desires and the limits of the "real world." You may find more discipline and focus available to you, coming from within.

Saturn Square/Quincunx Midheaven/IC

Power struggles are a danger in this locale, where you could go head-to-head with authority figures, and your desire to run the show is likely to conflict with another person's determination to take charge. Vocational competition or jockeying for more status could occur, and you might feel that an authority figure is constrictive, restrictive, dictatorial, demanding, and limiting. You're also likely to feel you don't have enough time to accomplish all you wish to or must do. Although you can be very dedicated and hard-working, you might feel torn between professional ambitions and private (domestic) responsibilities. Patience and realism are among your assets if you apply them well.

Saturn Square/Quincunx Ascendant/Descendant

You are likely to deal personally with issues of power and control, and may have to resist an overbearing authority figure or feel challenged by those who refuse to accept your commands. Responsibility is a key issue, with your challenge being to accept appropriate responsibility (not trying to dodge it) without taking on too much (carrying the load for everyone around you). Getting your career in gear is apt to be more challenging here, where more barriers or blockages seem to arise, and your inner critic could be stronger in this locale. You may work very hard here, perhaps even trying to balance two or more different career paths. Experience (sometimes the School of Hard Knocks) is a good teacher here, and you can put much effort into improving your status and honing your expertise.

Uranus

Uranus Conjunction Midheaven-Opposition IC

You might become a professional astrologer in this location, or be involved with computers, new technology, groups, organizations, progressive ideas, or anything on the cutting edge of change. A New Age focus is possible. Chaos and anarchy in the vocational realm is also an option. Sudden changes and abrupt breaks and shifts could occur. Perhaps authority figures are very unpredictable. Perhaps chaos reigns at the workplace. You could be ready to declare your independence from the workaday world and start your own career, or quit (or be fired), because of your independent attitude. You are apt to want more variety, intellectual stimulation, and personal freedom in your profession. Your challenge is to find a good balance between the old and the new and between conventional and unconventional approaches.

Uranus Conjunction IC-Opposition Midheaven

This is a very restless combination, and you will have trouble staying home unless you can fill your nest with Uranus-related experiences or people, including the unusual, new technology, humanitarian efforts, the unconventional, or insightful, creative activities. People with this placement often have to "run away from home" periodically. They easily feel too hemmed in or tied down. Chaos could reign within the domicile, and unexpected events occur often. Family members could be more erratic or unpredictable, and you are apt to develop more objectivity and tolerance of the foibles of others in this region. The need for variety, newness, and excitement is strong with Uranus, so it would be difficult to get the stability and security for which the fourth house of home and family yearns.

Uranus Conjunction Ascendant-Opposition Descendant

The *Star Trek* mantra comes to mind: "to boldly go where no one has gone before." Your unique, individualistic side is accented here. Rebellious or revolutionary tendencies could come out as the urge for freedom will be strengthened and deepened. You could become more inventive, innovative, unconventional, detached, humanitarian, progressive, eccentric, unusual, or erratic and unpredictable. It's also possible that you could become personally involved with astrology, new technology, or anything on the cutting edge of change. Your tolerance and open-mindedness may also increase.

Uranus Conjunction Descendant-Opposition Ascendant

You may attract people in this location who are unusual, unconventional, rebellious, progressive, or eccentric. Or, your relationships may feature abrupt changes, sudden shifts, and unexpected developments. Either you or your partner may feel the need to periodically "run away" from intimacy. On the positive side, you find it easy to take turns with others and are likely to be good friends with romantic partners, valuing each other's individuality.

Uranus Sextile/Trine Midheaven/IC

You may gain status or advance professionally in fits and starts, and vocational changes could be a bit abrupt or sudden. Unexpected developments may turn out in your favor, in part because your networking skills, independent thinking, unconventional attitudes, or strength with new technology could prove to be assets within your career. You can work well inside and outside the Establishment, and are likely to find a way to be both independent and efficient—perhaps seeking more power in order to gain additional freedom. Future trends are apt to be on your side, and you might receive assistance from friends or from groups or organizations in which you are active. You can brainstorm new ways to enhance your status or profession.

Uranus Sextile/Trine Ascendant-Descendant

You may become more future-oriented and interested in progressive prospects in this location, where it should be easier to express your unique and individualistic side. Your originality could increase because here you see multiple options and can envision lots of possibilities. An experimental attitude (testing and trying things out) serves you well. Others notice your eccentricity or unconventional behavior and are supportive. You get encouragement for your open-minded attitude, brainstorming skills, and sudden flashes of insight.

Uranus Square/Quincunx Midheaven/IC

You may rub authority figures the wrong way without meaning to because by just being yourself you're likely to clash with the powers that be in this region. You are apt to resist the rules, regulations, and established procedures that are in vogue here, and may become an outcast, an exile, an iconoclast whom others see as a rebel. Your desire for variety, excitement, and new experiences could make vocational stability a bit tougher to achieve. (You are more inclined to quit, be fired, or change jobs often.) Your challenge is to know when to follow the rules and when to break them, and which rules should be broken. Constant change and variety may be central in your vocation, or you may try to do several different things professionally. You also might work to change an existing structure (including your professional life) or go outside the Establishment and build your own, new, unique structure.

Uranus Square/Quincunx Ascendant/Descendant

You may feel that life is more abrupt or less predictable in this location. Perhaps friends are less stable or the groups with which you are involved go through many changes. Personal independence and unconventionality are highlighted, and your challenge is to avoid either extreme—too much (becoming the rebel without a cause) or too little (letting others co-opt you and keep you in narrow, conventional channels). Learning when to break the rules (and which ones to break) is essential. You may decide to make radical alterations in your physical appearance or body, and if you're accident-prone, this placement could exacerbate the tendency. An experimental, open-minded attitude will serve you best.

Neptune

Neptune Conjunction Midheaven-Opposition IC

In this area, you might gravitate toward fields that feature art, beauty, compassion, healing, escapism, or imagination. You could work in professions with magical, mystical, or visionary elements, and authority figures might be inspirational, sensitive, confused, sympathetic, or inclined to run away from reality. If the idealistic component of this combination is overdone, you could be disappointed and disillusioned in your professional choices. Careers may seem to dissolve, or you chronically search for that "perfect" situation that does not exist. The professional victim is one negative option. On the positive side, you can bring visions into form in an artistic medium. You could make the world better through helping people, particularly the downtrodden or less fortunate. You could offer people a glimpse of something higher, a transcendent experience.

Neptune Conjunction IC-Opposition Midheaven

You might find a home by the water in this location, or the ideal, lovely, and beautiful home. You will probably want your home to be a sanctuary, a safe retreat and arena from which you can shut out the world if you wish. A serene, attractive domestic environment is important. You will be more sensitive to where you live and the people (and pets) with whom you live, so surrounding yourself with positive influences is extra important. This combination can denote a "mother/savior" tendency whereby you give, and give, and give (too much) to other people in trying to help, heal, or make it all better for them. Problems with drugs, alcohol, or fantasy are possible for you and/or family members. Illusions and lies can be part of the downside. On the positive side, your creative imagination will be more fruitful. You can establish a richer spiritual life and share your idealism and visions with those closest to you.

Neptune Conjunction Ascendant-Opposition Descendant

You could become more graceful and physically attractive (enhance your appearance) in this location. Aesthetic abilities may increase, and a talent for grace in action (beautiful sports such as dancing, skating, tai chi, etc.) is highlighted. You may instinctively do the right thing at the right time, having been led by your inner wisdom. You are likely to be more sensitive physically and should be extra careful with drugs and alcohol. You may feel more imaginative, idealistic, intuitive, or confused, lost in fantasy, or prone to illusions and misconceptions. You could develop a more personal interest in healing or other compassionate pursuits.

Neptune Conjunction Descendant-Opposition Ascendant

Romance is in the air, and fairy tales reign supreme. The quest for a perfect, idyllic love is alive and well. This combination can seek (and imagine) the best in others, and can be in love with love or disillusioned when the rose-colored glasses come off. Fantasies of perfection and "happily ever after" could abound. Compassion is accentuated, and you might try to rescue partners from drugs, alcohol, illness, etc. If we expect other people to bring us "heaven on earth," we will be let down. This motif is best handled by sharing artistic interests and talents with others, or through philanthropic endeavors, mystical interests, and inspired activities.

Neptune Sextile/Trine Midheaven/IC

Your imagination, artistic abilities, intuition, or compassion could advance your career or enhance your status. Your graceful style may appeal to authority figures, and you can inspire the powers that be. You're able to bring the transcendent and mystical into form in the material world, and artistic and healing skills produce tangible results. You probably know when to go with the flow and when to take charge and direct the action. Visualization skills could be an important vocational asset.

Neptune Sextile/Trine Ascendant/Descendant

Your imaginative, compassionate side serves you well here. Perhaps your "invisible antennae" pick up vital impressions. Perhaps your idealistic, philanthropic instincts find favor in the eyes of others. Perhaps you do more with your creative imagination and artistic abilities. You also might do more rescuing or charitable work—aiding the less fortunate, ill, or downtrodden. Your faith and mystical connection to something higher could provide personal support, and you could be led to do the right thing at the right time. Your courage is fed by your faith, visions, and dreams, and you enjoy venturing into other dimensions, alternate aspects of reality.

Neptune Square/Quincunx Midheaven/IC

Your dreams and visions are apt to conflict with those of authority figures. Perhaps your perceptions of reality are truly different. Perhaps one (or both) of you has problems with drugs, alcohol, or fantasy. You are likely to feel torn between romantic, idealistic dreams and paying attention to the bottom line, and may be unsure when to dissolve boundaries and when to take control and work firmly within the limits. Your urge to help and heal others could be a professional asset, or could result in your feeling drained and exhausted. Your challenge is to find a healthy outlet for your desire to be inspired and uplifted, and to bring your dreams into form in the material world.

Neptune Square/Quincunx Ascendant/Descendant

Your physical sensitivity could increase here, so be extra careful with drugs, alcohol, and anything you put in your body. You may find it easier to succumb to "poor me" feelings (a victim attitude) and could be susceptible to feeling tired, drained, and overwhelmed. Excessive idealism (yearning for the impossible dream) can lead to disappointments. You might wear rose-colored glasses in relationships, inviting people to take advantage of you. You can become more graceful and attractive in this area, and you may become more active in creating beauty, sometimes literally with your physical body. Compassion is apt to increase. Your challenge is to find a happy medium between self-assertion and self-sacrifice.

Pluto

Pluto Conjunction Midheaven-Opposition IC

Power issues are front and center. You could be drawn to professions that involve joint resources (money, investments, etc.), intense emotions, life-and-death circumstances, or hidden matters, or those that require great forcefulness, concentration, and self-control. Business partnerships are quite possible. A practical attitude toward financial matters is likely. This combination can be rather compulsive, and you may have trouble letting go and moving on (tenacity could be overdone). If self-discipline is carried to the extreme, even reasonable indulgences may be eschewed. Self-denial is possible and could affect sensual and sexual interactions. Being your own boss or a mover, shaker, and doer is more important to you in this locale.

Pluto Conjunction IC-Opposition Midheaven

Your feelings could be more intense in this area, where you may have to deal with life-and-death matters in your domestic environment. You could become more secretive or hermitlike, retreating inside your own psyche and into the nest. A desire for control probably will be channeled toward your home, and could be directed toward family members. Power struggles, particularly over money, sexuality, possessions, and questions of who is in charge, are a possibility. On the down side, manipulation, emotional blackmail, and intimidation are all possible. (They might be directed toward you or your loved ones.) On the positive side, you may delve more deeply into occult studies, research, therapy, or ways and means to gain more self-mastery and self-control. Intense emotional bonds could form with family members or in a familial-type setting. Major emotional transformations are possible.

Pluto Conjunction Ascendant-Opposition Descendant

You could strengthen your physical body in this locale or do endurance or resistance training. Self-control and self-mastery move up on the priority list, and you might decide to stop smoking or drinking, improve your eating habits, or make other major transformations that require much concentration, discipline, and follow-through. Sexual issues could move into higher focus, as could sharing resources (money, possessions, pleasures) with an intimate partner. You could become personally involved with occult studies, life-and-death matters, or exploring the dark side and taboo areas. Therapy is an option. On the down side, ruthlessness and relentless behavior are possible. Being able to forgive, forget, and move on is apt to be somewhat challenging. Releasing and letting go may require extra effort. A do-or-die determination is likely.

Pluto Conjunction Descendant-Opposition Ascendant

Relationships are apt to be extra intense in this location, which means they can be very, very good or very, very bad. Emotional blackmail, manipulation, intimidation, and power struggles (particularly over sex and money) are possible. You might feel used and abused, or be inclined to do the same to others. On the positive side, you could attract individuals who operate like skilled therapists, encouraging you to know yourself more deeply and transform negative habit patterns into positive ones. You could build stamina and self-mastery through interactions with others.

Pluto Sextile/Trine Midheaven/IC

Organizational abilities, perseverance, concentration, self-control, and endurance are likely to contribute to your vocational success in this locale. Research abilities may be enhanced, and your dedication and thoroughness could impress authority figures. Loyalty is apt to be a major issue, and you are capable of making a strong commitment. On the down side, power struggles are possible with bosses, family members, and just about anyone. A spouse or mate may contribute to your success in the material world, and your ability to read nonverbal cues and look beneath the surface of life will help you in making pragmatic business decisions. You may find it easier to do fundraising, get loans, or use money to make money (investments). Business partnerships are possible. Counseling and consulting talents are probable.

Pluto Sextile/Trine Ascendant/Descendant

You may find it easier to share power, possessions, and pleasures with others in this locale, and intense emotions could become a positive rather than a problem. Your powers of transformation, particularly to replace negative habit patterns with positive ones, prove useful. Sexual intensity could increase, and you might find it easier to balance intimacy and a desire for independence. Your courage is tested and refined by exploring hidden areas and having the grit and determination to see things through, no matter how difficult, as endurance and perseverance are accentuated.

Pluto Square/Quincunx Midheaven/IC

This location may accent power struggles, and the struggle for control is quite possible. Arguments or strife may develop over issues of sex, joint resources (especially money), addictions, intense emotional reactions, secrets, or manipulative actions. You also could feel torn between professional responsibilities and the urge for intimacy, yet the potential for self-discipline is strong. It's also likely that you can unearth hidden factors and might receive a negative reaction when delivering unpalatable facts. Compromise is not easy with this combination, and the practice of forgiving and forgetting is important. You can hang on too long, particularly to negative emotions, and become obsessive. Learn to cleanse, release, and move on.

Pluto Square/Quincunx Ascendant/Descendant

Power is in high focus in this location, where you're challenged to work on owning your personal power and sharing it wisely with others. Therefore, issues of earning and owning are apt to be emphasized, and you may struggle over the partnership questions of who brings in the income or who calls the shots in terms of money, sexuality, and possessions. Intimacy instincts are stimulated, but so is the desire for independence, so compromises are essential. Emotions are likely to be intense in this locale, especially anger and resentment, which require extra care and handling. Being able to forgive and forget (yourself as well as others) is vital. In extreme cases, violence is possible. Your challenge is to develop your strong, forceful, tenacious side while respecting the rights of others.

5
Changing Ascendant Signs

When you relocate your chart, the signs on the angles of your horoscope shift, a little or a lot, depending upon how far you move from your birthplace. Even so, you never "lose" or replace your birth chart and all its pluses and minuses; it follows you wherever you go. You do, however, feel a subtle influence from the signs that are on the angles in another location. It's an opportunity to learn more about yourself and other signs, as well as to emphasize particular signs based on your own goals and desires.

Suppose, for example, you were born with a Virgo Ascendant and a chart that features many planets in earth and water signs; this combination can be somewhat shy and reticent. If reaching out socially is a little difficult for you, consider moving to a location that changes your Ascendant to a fire sign (Aries, Leo, Sagittarius) or an air sign (Gemini, Libra, Aquarius). You won't magically "leave behind" all your Virgo shyness and self-critical tendencies, but you can soften them and add an overlay that makes it easier for you to reach out to and enjoy other people.

When you change the sign on your Ascendant through relocation, you bring in a blend of the sign from your birth and the sign from the new location. The Ascendant/Descendant axis says much about your instinctive actions and personal style (how you present yourself to the outer world and how others view you) and how you relate to people, particularly in terms of one-on-one exchanges.

Here are some broad guidelines to use in interpreting Ascendant and Midheaven sign changes:

- If you want more personal confidence, energy, or initiative, put a fire sign (Aries, Leo, Sagittarius) on the Ascendant.
- If you want more pragmatism, ability to work effectively in the material world, or patience, put an earth sign (Taurus, Virgo, Capricorn) on the Ascendant.
- If you want improved communication skills, sociability, or objectivity, put an air sign (Gemini, Libra, Aquarius) on the Ascendant.
- If you want more sensitivity, intuition, or compassion, put a water sign (Cancer, Scorpio, Pisces) on the Ascendant.

Before continuing, here are a few examples to help illustrate the principles of the Ascendant changing signs:

- A woman who had a Cancer Ascendant in her birthplace horoscope was quite shy, retiring, and inward as a child. She moved to a location that gave her a Gemini Ascendant, and became much more outgoing, expressive, and communicative.
- Another woman was born with a Taurus Ascendant and a strong earth element influence in her chart. She moved west to where Aries was on the Ascendant in her relocated horoscope, and was much more physically active, assertive, and confident.
- A woman with a Capricorn Ascendant had a tough childhood and worked very hard even when quite young. She moved to an area that relocated her Ascendant to Sagittarius, and went a little wild for a little while, partying, celebrating, and goofing off a lot. Now, she is directing her Sagittarius Ascendant toward philosophy, metaphysics, education, and a search for truth.

Now identify the Ascendant sign in your birth chart. Do the same with your favorite locations, those under consideration for relocation, and anywhere you spent a significant amount of time during your childhood and teen years.

Next, find the section for your natal (birth) Ascendant in the following listings, and, within that section, read the information for the relocated Ascendant sign. Remember, both the Ascendant and the Descendant change signs.

Aries Natal Ascendant

Aries to Taurus

This shift highlights strength of will, active pursuit of pleasure, a persistent approach to issues of assertion, and satisfaction in doing one's own thing. More patience is possible. The relationship focus is deeper and more intense.

Aries to Gemini

Gemini emphasizes mental and verbal activities, thinking and communication centered around personal needs and desires, along with good eye-mind-hand coordination. You're expressive, alert, and eager for variety, and an adventurous motif emerges in relationships with a quest for inspiration and broadened horizons.

Aries to Cancer

Cancer influences Aries with an inner push/pull between personal needs and those of family members. Self-nurturing is likely, and you may become more protective of yourself and others. Old instincts toward separation and independence move toward forming emotional attachments, and questions of control versus sharing emerge in relationships. Learning to take turns with responsibility could be an issue.

Aries to Leo

This sign combination highlights vitality, energy, enthusiasm, and star power, and brings out an exuberance that is fun-loving, active, and full of zest and sparkle. You instinctively seek the center stage. An inventive, unconventional note enters the mix in interpersonal exchanges.

Aries to Virgo

Personal will becomes directed more toward work and productive results, and there may be a push/pull between speed and precision. Health interests could become more important. Idealistic urges ("in love with love") could spill into relationships. Sharing a dream with a partner works best.

Aries to Libra

"Me first" moves more toward "you first" with this combination, and the potential exists for an excellent balance between assertion and accommodation, between what you want and the desires of others. An interest in active forms of beauty (dancing, skiing, gymnastics, etc.) is quite possible.

Aries to Scorpio

Spontaneity is toned down, and impulses are moderated by looking beneath the surface and investigating deeply. Strong feelings are highlighted, sexuality may be enhanced, and the drive for independence could compete with the drive for intimacy. Personal will and power are highlighted, and resources and comfort become more of a priority in relationships.

Aries to Sagittarius

An adventurous motif is highlighted, and independence and a desire for thrills are accentuated. A questing theme could become significant, and you are extroverted, restless, and eager for more. Communication is central in relationships, and the urge for variety increases.

Aries to Capricorn

Personal will can encounter limitations (rules of the game of life). You're also ambitious, have a strong desire for control, and can put much energy into achieving your goals. Career and status thus become more central to self-expression and personal action, but speed vies with caution and planning. Mutual nurturing matters are prominent, and a partnership may become more like a parent-child exchange. Family matters have a strong influence in relationships.

Aries to Aquarius

Inventive, independent, rebellious, and resistant to any limitations, you're eager to go beyond traditional boundaries, and need a lot of space and personal freedom. You seek more excitement and thrills in relationships, and expect to maintain your free will. Too much togetherness can be smothering.

Aries to Pisces

Personal will becomes less central as idealistic or compassionate motifs gain ground in personal expression in this location. You're challenged to find a happy medium between self-assertion and self-sacrifice. Personal spiritual or mystical experiences become a higher priority. Graceful movement is likely. Common sense is highlighted in relationships.

Taurus Natal Ascendant

Taurus to Aries

Sensuality and the pursuit of personal desires is heightened, and the focus tends to be immediate, only on the present. You may be self-indulgent in this location, and former couch potatoes become more active. Sharing and caring are accentuated in relationships.

Taurus to Gemini

You seek pleasure through the world of the mind, and gratification is tied to thinking and communicating. Sensible about the everyday activities and events, you're interested in and discuss different avenues of sensual satisfaction. Depth and breadth are pursued in relationships.

Taurus to Cancer

In this location you're more tactile and oriented toward safety and security, both physically and emotionally. You find pleasure in domestic connections and may collect things, while also enjoying home, family, and emotional ties. Issues of power and control emerge with other people. Sharing the authority is key.

Taurus to Leo

Determination and strong willpower are emphasized, and you may feel torn between playing it safe and taking a few risks. You're eager to indulge yourself and loved ones, and have a strong sensual/sexual streak in this location, where loyalty is accentuated. Relationships range from emotionally intense to coolly detached.

Taurus to Virgo

Very sensible, grounded, and pragmatic in this location, you may focus more on work, which could be tied to beauty or material goods. You're patient and thorough, and healthy habits start to prevail over self-indulgence. Feelings are accentuated in relationships; beware of "needing to be needed" and attracting people who need help. Sensitivity reigns in one-on-one exchanges.

Taurus to Libra

You have a more relaxed, affable, friendly style in this location, where you shy away from "making waves." But you also can go out of your way to avoid unpleasantness. A strong personal connection to beauty and aesthetics is indicated, and you may have increased personal charm and/or physical attractiveness. A push/pull is possible in relationships; find a happy medium between sharing and the desire for separation and independence.

Taurus to Scorpio

Sensuality and sexuality are emphasized, and there can be swings to the extreme (feast versus famine) with food, alcohol, spending, etc. Strong loyalty and much patience and perseverance are likely. Issues of "yours, mine, and ours" tend to come up in relationships.

Taurus to Sagittarius

Comfort and ease are less of a priority than escapades and new horizons. The mundane and material moves toward the spiritual or inspirational, and the urge for independence moves you past former comfort zones. More lighthearted moments arise in relationships, and intensity lessens. Communication may improve.

Taurus to Capricorn

Common sense is accentuated, and productive accomplishments are likely. You have a heightened appreciation of life's material goodies, and responsibility, patience, and follow-through are strong. Parental motifs can affect one-on-one exchanges. Be sure that strengths are shared and responsibilities are fairly divided.

Taurus to Aquarius

A fresh approach to financial matters and sensual pleasures is possible, but you may feel torn between protecting the status quo and seeking excitement and new experiences. You might be ready to change your "look" and style, and drama is on the rise in relationships. Strong wills are in focus in interpersonal exchanges. The thrill factor increases.

Taurus to Pisces

You're more idealistic about pleasure, finances, and comfort. Kind and gentle, you also could be passive or too inclined to avoid unpleasantness. There are strong feelings for beauty, as well as the potential to realize artistic ability, and you might take steps to become more attractive. Others may prove hard-working and competent or critical and judgmental. Shared tasks help keep the critical factor at bay in relationships.

Gemini Natal Ascendant

Gemini to Aries

Personal independence is on the rise. Doing your own thing is more important, and you have a quick wit and glib tongue. Repartee and debating skills are likely. Boredom comes easily, so lots of diverse activities and interests are likely. Relationships move toward more equality, and togetherness gains appeal over separate feats.

Gemini to Taurus

Casual conversations move toward sensually satisfying exchanges, and an enlarged desire for comfort and stability is likely. Personal pursuit of money (and resources) could increase, and thoughts may focus on finances, comfort, and gratification. Relationships are apt to become a bit more intense, with a willingness to dig and look beneath the surface.

Gemini to Cancer

Feelings gain precedence over intellect in this location, where domestic or family matters increase in personal importance. Security-seeking has a higher priority, and you place a higher value on predictability and dependability in relationships. Your love of variety is influenced and, at times, outweighed by the desire for safety and protection.

Gemini to Leo

An outgoing focus continues. If you're an excellent communicator, you could become a natural entertainer (the bon vivant). Amusing, vibrant, and versatile, you could be more flirtatious. Exploits and new experiences are highlighted in relationships, and an attraction to independent types is likely.

Gemini to Virgo

Your strong mental focus is rational and objective, and interests may shift from quantity to quality, from verbal communication to written. Work and health move up on the personal priority list. Idealism and high standards reign in the relationship realm, but beware of wanting more than is possible or succumbing to the view through rose-colored glasses. Shared dreams work well.

Gemini to Libra

Interacting with other people and sharing ideas are emphasized, and your lighthearted style becomes more charming and diplomatic. Casual connections can be deepened. In this location you could be a natural mixer, socially and professionally, and eager to share. Relationships feature an attraction to energetic, outgoing individuals.

Gemini to Scorpio

Increased intensity is likely, and deeper self-analysis is probable as a desire for variety gives way to a determination to see things through and to be thorough. Communication could take on a sarcastic, biting edge, and curiosity about taboo subjects and hidden matters increases. Priorities in relationships shift from escapades, travel, and inspiration to sensual pleasures, comfort, and stability.

Gemini to Sagittarius

Communication is accentuated, and a sense of humor is likely in this location. This extroverted combination favors travel, education (as student or as teacher), and all kinds of new experiences. Restlessness remains strong, however, and a love of variety continues in the relationship realm.

Gemini to Capricorn

Your lighthearted style becomes more sober and serious in this location, as responsibility and realism move up on the priority list. Controlled communication is a likely goal, and casual gives way to concentration and focus. Adventure, exploration, and freedom in relationships morph into a desire for more safety, emotional support, and familiarity.

Gemini to Aquarius

Ideas and people are in high focus with this combination, and innovative thinking is enhanced. An unconventional bent enters the mix, and you seek unusual opportunities and activities. Communication and mental stimulation are vital to your well-being, and relationships center on a desire for action and excitement.

Gemini to Pisces

In this location you blend your casual communication style with an empathetic one as mind and heart are combined. A tendency to have multiple interests and activities continues, however, so it would be easy to scatter your forces. Personal beautification is an option, and you may hold yourself to a higher standard. Relationships that had emphasized frolic and exploration focus more on productivity sand competence.

Cancer Natal Ascendant

Cancer to Aries

Your inward, safety-seeking focus shifts to a more confident, independent style, and you gain a stronger sense of self and a willingness to put yourself first. Taking care of "me" gains precedence over taking care of others. Relationships that featured motifs of mastery, control, power, and responsibility move toward more equality and sharing.

Cancer to Taurus

The emotional undertone in your personality becomes more relaxed and pragmatic. In essence, you become more comfortable in your own skin, like yourself better, and are able to indulge sensually. Money and possessions are higher personal priorities now, and relationships highlight issues of control and mastery, with increased depth and intimacy as potentials.

Cancer to Gemini

Your somewhat shy personality becomes more outgoing and communicative, and your family focus shifts to the world of the mind. Flexibility and versatility also increase, and relationships move from a focus on control and responsibility to a love of exploration, enlightenment, ideas, ideals, and far horizons.

Cancer to Leo

Your inward, cautious style becomes more extroverted and outgoing, and personal risk-taking and thrill-seeking are likely to increase. This combination is usually family-oriented, warm, and eager to love and be loved. Relationships move from control and predictability to looking for exploits, new experiences, and unconventional possibilities.

Cancer to Virgo

Emotional nurturing and protection move toward physical competence and caretaking. But this tends to be a very "helpful" combination, and you could carry too much of the load, emotionally and in terms of tasks. The practical demands of the working world become as important as domestic goals, and an element of imagination, fantasy, idealism, or inspiration enters into relationships.

Cancer to Libra

The desire for justice and equality becomes more predominant in this location. Parental motifs in relationships shift more toward sharing and taking turns, but some time/energy competition between family needs and the desires of a partner is possible. Shyness is overlaid with diplomatic skills, and more action and excitement are possible in relationships.

Cancer to Scorpio

Your internal focus remains prominent in this location, as does the tendency to check your inner voice before saying or doing anything. Self-control becomes even more important here, and relationships that feature pragmatism, responsibility, and work move toward more indulgence and pleasure.

Cancer to Sagittarius

If you're shy and security-seeking, you could become more adventurous and outgoing, and travel, far horizons, education, truth-seeking, or other inspirational activities are more appealing. Relationships become more varied, and mental matters and communication gain precedence over practical concerns. You might broaden your domestic environment or expand your family ties (or close, emotional attachments).

Cancer to Capricorn

Your warm, nurturing personal style becomes more guarded and controlled, and work or practical concerns take precedence over domestic ones. Parental motifs are strong in partnerships, where the goal is to take turns taking care of each other. Do not allow one person to carry the whole load emotionally or in terms of real-world demands. Old, unfinished business with parents could pop up in relationships.

Cancer to Aquarius

If you're naturally somewhat shy and retiring, you become more expressive and willing to break the rules in this location. An unconventional note enters the mix, and mental mastery takes over from emotional reactivity. Relationships highlight issues of "Who's in charge?" There is an increased desire for excitement and contact with unusual people.

Cancer to Pisces

In this location sensitivity and compassion are doubly emphasized. With this combination you can be somewhat reticent or hesitant, fearful of being hurt or hurting others, as the emphasis is on being protective and protected. Relationships emphasize practical matters, and issues of work and competence are in high focus with other people.

Leo Natal Ascendant

Leo to Aries

Vitality and action are highlighted in this location, where drama becomes less important than the freedom to pursue your own path. Excitement is the breath of life, and you seek thrills, while movement, initiative, and confidence are accented. Relationships emphasize ideas and people, with an increased focus on sharing and taking turns with others.

Leo to Taurus

Your natural stage presence is subdued and morphs into a more relaxed, sensual style, although performing (as a part of everyday life or professionally) is still pleasurable. Comfort, reliability, and predictability become more of a priority, as does acquiring resources and money. A strong sensual/sexual emphasis is present, but relationships are likely to accentuate the tension between intimacy and a desire for personal space and freedom. Compromise is essential.

Leo to Gemini

With this combination you're quite extroverted, laugh a lot, and enjoy entertaining others with your amusing way with words. Persuasive communication is probable in this location, which can positively influence your professional and personal lives. Relationships highlight stretching boundaries, seeking new experiences, experimentation, and escapades.

Leo to Cancer

In this location you, the natural leader, mover, and shaker, gain more compassion and the ability to quietly nurture others. Loving warmth is emphasized, and domestic matters become more important. Issues of safety and protection (of self and others) are highlighted, and relationships move from a freewheeling emphasis to a desire for predictability, stability, and control.

Leo to Virgo

You become more studious, hard-working, or focused on health and healing in this location, as your extroverted, fun-loving style shifts to a greater concern with efficiency and practicality. Significant accomplishments are likely. Relationships get a little "fairy dust," with more focus on dreams, visions, fantasy, beauty, imagination, or ideals.

Leo to Libra

This combination merges the natural entertainer with the born diplomat, and you can become a real charmer! In this location you know what people want to hear and see and can provide it, and your charisma quotient is high. But guard against being too susceptible to opinions or wanting approval. Relationships emphasize independence and freedom, so some push/pull is likely between loving connections and having your own space.

Leo to Scorpio

An iron will is indicated in this location, and a forceful nature is highlighted. Some inner tension is possible between risk-taking urges and a desire for security. The drive for love and intimacy is strong, and passions are intense. Relationships that formerly featured independence and unconventionality move more toward comfort, sensual pleasures, and stability.

Leo to Sagittarius

Excitement is the name of the game in this location, and you likely have a fiery, extroverted style that's gregarious and friendly. A love of thrills and a willingness to take risks for greater gain are featured, but try not to go out on a limb. Relationships emphasize communication, mental stimulation, and fresh ideas.

Leo to Capricorn

Power issues are central, so finding a place to lead and take charge is vital. Your dramatic personal style becomes more disciplined and controlled, and, although love and romance remain important, ambition and accomplishment move up on the priority list. An attraction to independent, unconventional individuals shifts toward a desire for more safety and security in relationships.

Leo to Aquarius

Polarities reign in this location. Within yourself and your relationships, your challenge is to find a balance between being passionate versus intellectual detachment; being special versus being equal; being close and caring versus being independent. Swings and extremes are possible until a happy medium is achieved, and mutual appreciation works wonders.

Leo to Pisces

You, the natural entertainer, shift more toward the natural mystic. The extroverted side of your personality becomes quieter, and at times you retreat from the world. Empathy and compassion are on the rise, and, with increased persuasive skills, you could "cast a spell" on your audience. Creative and artistic abilities are apt to be strong, and pragmatism, service, and efficiency become more important in relationships.

Virgo Natal Ascendant

Virgo to Aries

Efficiency and speed are emphasized in this location, where you learn to do things more quickly but with the same precision. Your orientation toward humble service could shift toward putting yourself first more often as you gain confidence. Somewhat nebulous or dreamy tendencies in relationships diminish as equality and sharing become more of a priority.

Virgo to Taurus

The material world and its wealth become more important as you, the worker bee, learn to enjoy physical pleasures and possessions. Humble service shifts toward a focus on comfort, sensuality, and gratification. Common sense remains accented, and your style is likely to be practical, persistent, and systematic. Relationships emphasize tuning in to feelings and looking beneath the surface.

Virgo to Gemini

You broaden your life role of efficiency expert and learn multitasking; or, you feel completely scattered and distracted. The "quantity versus quality" dilemma is likely to come up in this location, because Gemini wants to do everything and Virgo wants to do everything well; compromise is essential. A talent for collecting and disseminating information is probable, and relationships highlight ideals and imagination.

Virgo to Cancer

Caretaking remains a strong drive, and your Virgo service orientation receives an additional overlay of maternal, nurturing instincts. The tendency is thus a "need to be needed," to look after others and to try to "fix" things (whether others want that or not). Practical problem-solving is applied to domestic matters. Partners are apt to be sensitive, secretive, or intuitive.

Virgo to Leo

If you're a hesitant, often self-critical Virgo, you gain more charisma and confidence in this location. Here, you emerge from your role as a humble, behind-the-scenes worker to earn praise and the chance to be front and center, gaining applause and admiration. Work is no longer the top priority; love and romance move up on the list. Relationships have a transpersonal, inspirational, or humanitarian bent.

Virgo to Libra

Your tendency to be a shy, self-critical worker gets the benefit of the more sociable and diplomatic Libra in this location. Pragmatic concerns become less of a focus as relationships move to the forefront. This combination can be competent and charming, but you may gather too much data and put off decision-making. Partners are apt be more outgoing and dynamic.

Virgo to Scorpio

Your noted common sense acquires emotional overtones, and a practical attitude might be applied to the realm of intimacy and joint resources. Analytical ability and research skills are accentuated, but guard against a compulsive trait that emerges. Determined productivity is a keynote, and relationships bring in the polarity of comfort and relaxation. Enjoy the moment.

Virgo to Sagittarius

Your reserved, humble approach to life becomes more gregarious, expressive, and adventurous in this location. A focus on details expands to include the big picture, and your confidence rises. A realist, you find a visionary focus, and pragmatism benefits from idealism. Relationships emphasize variety and multiple interests.

Virgo to Capricorn

Work remains a strong focus in this location, where the emphasis is on a practical, matter-of-fact approach, responsibility, and doing what needs to be done—thoroughly and completely. But, self-critical tendencies could be strengthened because you feel strong and confident when productivity rises. Tenderness and a maternal motif are experienced through relationships.

Virgo to Aquarius

You discover more of your individuality and independence in this location, which modifies your reticent, hard-working nature. Ideas and people move up on your priority list, and you're likely to shake up former routines and habits with unconventional approaches. The emphasis is on logic and objectivity, but the relationship focus is on imagination and the quest for thrills.

Virgo to Pisces

Your realistic side becomes more idealistic, and your pragmatic approach benefits from more compassion. On the down side, too much perfectionism is possible; on the positive side, you can work hard to make your dreams come true and to create a more beautiful or perfect world. This combination favors the artist or healer. Shared visions are possible in relationships, but also an overemphasis on perfectionism.

Libra Natal Ascendant

Libra to Aries

Your nature is to accommodate others, but this location gives you the opportunity to develop assertiveness skills; and pleasing partners, while still enjoyable, gives way to pleasing yourself. Initiative is also on the rise, and you become more willing to make the first move. Your task is to learn to balance togetherness and your own needs, to take the personal space you need.

Libra to Taurus

An indulgent approach to life is likely in this location, where pleasure is a priority. A comfortable lifestyle is important, and you're even more attracted to art and beautiful objects. However, materialism and money matters may claim more of your attention than relationships, and partners are likely to be very strong willed and possessive.

Libra to Gemini

Communication remains highlighted in your life, and you continue to have a way with words. Your natural diplomatic nature might become more lighthearted and witty, with an emphasis on humor, and objectivity could increase. The ability to collect and disseminate information is accentuated. Fun, liveliness, and conversation accent close relationships.

Libra to Cancer

A protective tendency is emphasized in this location, where you go out of your way to avoid being emotionally hurt, and take the same approach with others. Caution is uppermost in guiding your personal style and decision-making, and family matters could claim more of your attention on a daily basis. Safety, security, and status are the goals in relationships.

Libra to Leo

Your personal charisma quotient is on the rise, and your people-pleasing talents get a boost from dramatic and persuasive skills. You excel at entertaining others in social and business situations, and capture more attention wherever you go. Adventure and independence are highlighted in relationships, and networking becomes one of your paths to success.

Libra to Virgo

Relationships move out of the forefront as work (and/or health) becomes more of a motivation in your life. The focus is on earthy, pragmatic concerns, particularly a desire for productivity. But, self-critical tendencies could increase, so be kind to yourself. You stress efficiency when dealing with other people, and craftsmanship skills could become a strength.

Libra to Scorpio

You, the natural diplomat, become somewhat more ruthless and tenacious, and people-pleasing skills become less important than digging up the facts, both pleasant and unpleasant. You also might face and master the dark side of life. Both competition and cooperation are highlighted in relationships, which accent comfort and material success more than excitement.

Libra to Sagittarius

Already noted for your agreeable nature, in this location you become even more outgoing, even gregarious, and the desire for adventure increases. Charm, charisma, and magnetism are probable, and a passion for justice is likely. The quest for mental stimulation, knowledge, and fresh horizons is highlighted. Variety and adventure appeal to you in close relationships.

Libra to Capricorn

Relationships may move down on your priority list, while professional ambitions move up. The balancing act between love and work is highlighted, and protocol, appropriate behavior, and a conservative approach are likely to be valued. Issues of control, authority, and caretaking become more central in relationships, as does increased responsibility.

Libra to Aquarius

Ideas and people remain a primary focus in this location, but your tendency to want to please everyone can evolve into more independence in thought and deed. Objectivity, tolerance, communication, and a friendly attitude are probable. The quest for excitement and thrills in relationships is heightened, and you attract unusual, stimulating people and situations.

Libra to Pisces

A soft, gentle style is accented in this location, where your tactful approach is an asset. But the possibility also exists for many "little white lies" and stretching the truth. Aesthetic talents are probable, and art, music, and mysticism attract you. Sociable instincts are watered down, however, and solitude is more appealing. In relationships, practical matters receive more emphasis.

Scorpio Natal Ascendant

Scorpio to Aries

A feisty motif is highlighted in this location, where you're willing to fight for what you want. Here, the careful, in-depth, and well-planned nature of your Scorpio Ascendant is willing to accept a bit more impulsive behavior. But you also might be prone to emotional swings—or even explosions. Comfort, togetherness, and partnership are accented in relationships.

Scorpio to Taurus

Your strong self-control eases toward self-indulgence. There could be some "feast versus famine" swings (dieting versus overeating; drinking versus not drinking; smoking versus not smoking; sex versus celibacy; spending versus saving, etc.) until you achieve a happy medium. You and a partner may battle with these issues, and emotional intensity gets an overlay of common sense. Moderation is the goal.

Scorpio to Gemini

Your intense, all-or-nothing personal style becomes lighter and less obsessive. A fascination with hidden matters shifts to an interest in anything and everything as well as a love of learning. Secrets are no longer paramount; open communication is valued. A blend of the profound and flippant is likely. Relationships accent comfortable adventures, risk for greater material gain, or establishing a spiritual base.

Scorpio to Cancer

Strong feelings and emotions are highlighted, and protective instincts become more important in your life, including personal and family safety and security. Reticence is likely, and silence can be used as a weapon. Domestic concerns take on added emphasis, and common sense and practicality are emphasized in the relationship realm.

Scorpio to Leo

Power motifs and leadership skills are highlighted as you, the behind-the-scenes manipulator or politician, emerge, ready for the limelight, eager for attention and applause. A forceful nature is likely, and your sexual drive and charisma could intensify. Mood swings (up and down) are probable. Security-versus-risk issues trigger relationship tension, but partners bring fresh ideas and excitement.

Scorpio to Virgo

Tenacity pays off with efficiency and productivity, and a do-or-die attitude serves you well in the workaday world, allowing you to hang in there and get the job done well. Self-critical tendencies might increase, so try not to become obsessed with your faults. Research and organizational skills are emphasized. Listen when partners encourage you to relax.

Scorpio to Libra

Intensity can be softened with diplomatic, tactful people-pleasing skills in this location, where relationships are in high focus and joint resources are an arena for discussion. Striving for and reaching comfortable compromise with others is highlighted; emphasize give-and-take with other people, professionally and personally. Sharing power is a significant motif.

Scorpio to Sagittarius

Your deep (and at times brooding) soul is more outgoing here, where your noted "poker face," and the life approach it represents, becomes more open and forthright, with a willingness to go with the flow. Your intense emotions benefit from a philosophical overlay and the quest for intellectual adventures. Communication and curiosity are more pivotal in relationships.

Scorpio to Capricorn

Power remains a central issue, including questions concerning rules, expectations, and who's in charge, and personal responsibility becomes paramount. Goals and ambitions are highlighted, because this combination signifies a thorough, relentless, disciplined approach, as well as the motivation to aim for the top. Here, you prefer a comfortable, supportive partner.

Scorpio to Aquarius

Your tendency to become overly absorbed (even obsessed) could be tempered with some objectivity. However, your interest could swing back and forth between intense intimacy and a cool, detached, independent style. Relationships feature the push/pull between safety and risk-taking, or stability and change, as well as ego and friendship issues.

Scorpio to Pisces

Emotions are highlighted in this location, where secrets could abound and activity goes on beneath the surface. You're reluctant to reveal too much to others and may adopt a mysterious "aura" to avoid giving away too much information. An element of compassion is added, and the urge to merge is strong; but you can withdraw as a protective measure. Partnerships highlight common sense.

Sagittarius Natal Ascendant

Sagittarius to Aries

Confidence and action are accentuated (and could be overdone to the point of rash behavior), and you are eager to do your own thing in the world. Freedom beckons strongly. You need adventure and excitement and are a natural self-starter. Relationships emphasize communication, sociability, and bouncing ideas back and forth.

Sagittarius to Taurus

The natural extravagance and outreach of Sagittarius is brought down to earth in Taurus. A more practical approach is possible, and financial matters are likely to be given more weight. Adventure and the open road are less appealing, and the desire for security, stability, and comfort rises. Commitment, intensity, and focus in relationships become more appealing than variety.

Sagittarius to Gemini

Restlessness and curiosity are accented, and this combination emphasizes learning, teaching, and traveling. You could be the perpetual student, eager traveler, or natural teacher. Boredom comes rather easily, so you should seek lots of mental stimulation and new experiences. Articulate, bright partners are preferred.

Sagittarius to Cancer

Sagittarius' focus on freedom shifts to a desire for the emotional closeness of Cancer. Home, family, roots, and safety gain priority over exploration and adventure. Your faith and beliefs can inspire loved ones, and your optimism is a boon to your nearest and dearest. Relationships are more serious, more "real," and more earnest (less lighthearted).

Sagittarius to Leo

Action, excitement, and thrills are on your agenda, because this eager, enthusiastic combination needs to move and craves the tingling and tumult of uproar and dramatic happenings. Confidence is likely to be high, and you can be a great coach, cheerleader, motivator, and wheeler-dealer who is able to persuade others. Relationships feature many ideas and mental stimulation.

Sagittarius to Virgo

Your idealistic urges are grounded with common sense and hard work, and you put sweat equity into manifesting your visions. This combination can be the practical idealist or the realistic mystic, so tread carefully until you know which. You also can be a perfectionist with yourself and in relationships. You are likely to work for your beliefs and values.

Sagittarius to Libra

This combination is quite magnetic. You're likely to find it easy to charm people in this location, most of whom find you attractive. A passion for justice and equality is possible, and you tend to expect the best of people—perhaps too much at times. Your friendly, outgoing nature helps you make great connections with just about anyone.

Sagittarius to Scorpio

Depth and breadth are combined. You see the overview, the big picture, and also dig beneath the surface. But you're apt to become more reticent as your natural bluntness is moderated by a tendency to keep secrets and reveal little. Freedom urges are overlaid with a desire for intimacy and soul connections. A focus on variety in relationships shifts toward a desire for stability and comfort.

Sagittarius to Capricorn

You can achieve more follow-through by adding an element of focus and concentration to your natural confidence. In this location you learn to bring your visions into material form by working in practical, productive ways to manifest your dreams. If the judgmental potential of Capricorn is overdone, you could feel frustrated. Safety is a higher priority in relationships.

Sagittarius to Aquarius

The lure of adventure and independence is intensified. An outgoing, future-oriented perspective is likely. You easily see the big picture, and could be concerned and involved in the pursuit of justice. The urge to explore is accentuated, and a mental emphasis is strong. In this location you can attract dramatic, magnetic, larger-than-life people.

Sagittarius to Pisces

Idealism is intensified, but you may feel torn between a blunt, honest approach and the desire to be kind—to save people's feelings with "polite lies." You are likely to seek personal, mystical experiences or look for answers about ultimate meaning. Self-expectations are apt to be high (perhaps too high), and moderation could be a challenge. Mental mastery and a drive for competence are featured in relationships.

Capricorn Natal Ascendant

Capricorn to Aries

If you have self-critical tendencies, there is the potential here for more confidence and initiative. You're more willing to put yourself first and pursue your own needs; guilt is not such a heavy load. The desire to be productive and responsible remains, but you will want to do things your own way. Parental themes in relationships give way to a desire for more equality and partnerships.

Capricorn to Taurus

Earthy matters—comfort, security, making a living, taking care of business—are doubly accented. You are apt to be reliable, responsible, predictable, and stable in this location, where self-critical tendencies are softened by the real potential to like yourself more and more. Relationships emphasize intuition, emotions, and looking beneath the surface.

Capricorn to Gemini

You can be more lighthearted in this locale, as your serious, sober, hard-working side gives way to an easygoing attitude that loves learning and a wide variety of experiences. Although accomplishment is still a personal priority, you're more willing to stop and smell the flowers, to explore many different options. You're also ready to be more adventurous and exploratory in relationships.

Capricorn to Cancer

Parental motifs are strong, and the desire for security is accentuated. Partnerships could become parent-child interactions, with one person having more of the power. To ensure equality, take turns filling the nurturing role and being the responsible one. You're very aware of striving to balance your time and energy between productive efforts in the outer world and domestic duties and demands.

Capricorn to Leo

Leadership skills are accented; you want to be in charge, running the show with flair and drama. You can sparkle while being practical and productive, and are likely to seek career recognition. Self-critical tendencies are mitigated, and you gain greater confidence. You're willing to take more risks, to break the rules in relationships rather than always playing it safe.

Capricorn to Virgo

Common sense remains a high priority, and the emphasis is on work, productivity, efficiency, and getting tangible results. This is a very dedicated, disciplined combination, but you also could overdo self-critical tendencies. Direct flaw-finding toward the physical world, not yourself. Relationships accent warmth, sensitivity, empathy, and support.

Capricorn to Libra

Love is on nearly equal footing with work in this location. Your desire is to find a better balance between practical duties and relationships, and ambition is influenced by your need for a more well-rounded lifestyle. Rather than play the critical parent, you are eager to be a true partner, and to learn to relax more, treat yourself more kindly, and appreciate appearance as well as functionality.

Capricorn to Scorpio

Intensity remains accentuated, and perseverance is a strong theme. What you set your mind upon, you are likely to accomplish. Good research and organizational skills are probable, as is business acumen, and a drive for power, mastery, and control is emphasized. Comfort, pleasure, and protection are highlighted in relationships.

Capricorn to Sagittarius

A serious, sober, hard-working theme wanes, balanced by laughter, extroversion, and adventure. You're eager to expand your horizons. Work is less a priority, and intellectual stimulation and new vistas become more important. Security in relationships also is less of a priority, while fresh ideas and insights become more important. You want bright partners who are good communicators.

Capricorn to Aquarius

You're more willing to break the rules now, and can think outside the box. Self-critical tendencies are probably lessened, and you have a greater appreciation for your unique qualities. Tradition and progress are a comfortable blend, and you can work inside and outside the Establishment. Relationships feature more drama and excitement.

Capricorn to Pisces

The hard-nosed, bottom-line focus of Capricorn is softened by sensitivity and empathy. An idealistic element enters the mix, as does an expanded imagination. Your instinctive realism can be applied to mystical, healing, or aesthetic matters, and you pursue your dreams in a responsible fashion. A protective motif is prevalent in relationships. Working with partners is an option.

Aquarius Natal Ascendant

Aquarius to Aries

Action and adventure become more appealing, and independence is accentuated by the desire to live life on your own terms. You can break new ground and be a pioneer. Courageous and innovative, your rebellious instincts might lead to rashness on occasion, and stimulation and variety satisfy you. Partners are apt to be quite magnetic and attractive—real charmers.

Aquarius to Taurus

A mental focus is grounded in the practical world. You put ideas to work, or earn money from them. Independence and excitement take a back seat to security and comfort, and loyalty and determination are accented. Your task is to maintain the status quo while embracing progress. Partners encourage you to share, and quality time is emphasized. Give priority to relationship issues.

Aquarius to Gemini

Curiosity and an eager, questing mind are accented, and you're interested in anything and everything. Lots of mental stimulation is essential to prevent boredom. Versatility and multiple talents are probable, and you need lots of variety and opportunities to learn and share information with others. Excitement and action are featured in relationships.

Aquarius to Cancer

Your focus on freedom is softened by a desire for emotional connections, but some push/pull is possible between devotion to family versus friends, or nesting activities versus exploring the wider world. You can be innovative in domestic matters, and supportive and nurturing of each family member's intellectual adventures. Power motifs are strong in relationships; avoid dominating or being dominated. Look for ways in which each person can be strong and in charge of his or her own arena.

Aquarius to Leo

Excitement is a strong drive, as is the desire for thrills and the rush of adrenaline. Your cool style becomes more passionate, and loving and being loved move up on the priority list; independence is not quite so essential as it was. You gravitate toward opportunities to shine, to earn admiration and applause. Relationships feature the freedom-versus-closeness dilemma and a balancing act between passion and detachment.

Aquarius to Virgo

Theory is brought down to earth and tested in the real world, as abstract concepts are measured against material facts. You're likely to do well at problem-solving and are able to think both in a linear, step-by-step fashion and in bursts and spurts of genius. A chaotic, rebellious personal style becomes more orderly and effective. Relationships become more subtle and mysterious, and less open and dramatic.

Aquarius to Libra

People and ideas are accented, and a sociable bent is likely. A strong drive for equality and fair play is present, and communication and objectivity rise high on the priority list. The desire for personal independence is softened as the urge for partnership and sharing becomes stronger. You are apt to attract others who are active, self-confident, and expressive.

Aquarius to Scorpio

Freedom urges give way to a strong desire for intimacy, but there could be some inner conflict before you find a happy medium. Your challenge here is to balance objective detachment and emotional intensity. There is an increased interest in seeing things through and in getting to the bottom of issues. Comfort and stability become higher priorities in relationships.

Aquarius to Sagittarius

Independence remains a major priority, and a lust for adventure is likely. You're willing to go where no one has gone before. A bright, quick mind is an asset in envisioning future possibilities, and you can inspire others. Friendly and extroverted, you can relate to anyone and everyone. Relationships feature humor, mental agility, and a love of variety.

Aquarius to Capricorn

Your rebellious, freedom-loving side can put on a three-piece suit and enter the Establishment in this location. Although you remain innovative, you do better working within the system, following the rules, and dealing with protocol. Achievement and making your mark in the world become more important, even though you retain that inner streak of eccentricity. Commitment matters more in relationships.

Aquarius to Pisces

Humanitarian instincts are strengthened, and your cool (even aloof) personal style becomes more sensitive and empathic. You may beautify yourself or become more personally active in mystical, artistic, or healing pursuits. Relationships move from the dramatic and passionate to the pragmatic and practical. Romance attracts you.

Pisces Natal Ascendant

Pisces to Aries

Increased confidence and extroversion are likely, and your initiative also could increase. Although much compassion and empathy remain, a greater degree of independence is possible. You can put beauty in motion and are likely to be assertive on behalf of the greater good. Relationships accent sharing more, and work and criticism less. Partners can be quite charming.

Pisces to Taurus

Going with the flow is a priority, and a strong desire exists for ease and comfort. There is a tendency to avoid unpleasantness, because this combination can be a bit passive or indulgent. Artistic skills and an attractive appearance are probable, and a kind demeanor likely. Partners emphasize competence, stamina, and seeing things through. (They might be a bit compulsive.) Endurance is highlighted.

Pisces to Gemini

Multiple interests can lead to being scattered. Diversity appeals, and an inner clash between intuition and logic is possible. You may use language with grace and beauty, and inspired communication is possible. If you're shy and retiring, expect to become more sociable. Relationships that emphasized work and critical judgment move toward adventure, exploration, and idealistic pursuits.

Pisces to Cancer

Gentleness is accentuated, as is a strong desire to assist others. Don't go overboard, however, into extremes of martyrdom or excessive dependency. Emotions are in high focus, and physical sensitivity is likely as well. Artistic inclinations are apt to be directed toward the nest. A pragmatic motif is predominant in relationships, and working with a partner is an option.

Pisces to Leo

Dramatic gestures are likely, and your creative imagination is backed up with flair and verve. This is an excellent combination for sales, promotions, or artistic activities. If you're shy, you can become more outgoing and expressive, with an active social life. Partners may seem more cool and detached. Logic is highlighted in relationships.

Pisces to Virgo

This sign duo does well in healing and helping fields as well as crafts and art, because the visionary, idealistic potentials of Pisces are backed up with the common sense, dedication, and efficiency of Virgo. You can become a realistic idealist or a pragmatic dreamer.

On the down side, cosmic discontent, perfectionism, or procrastination are dangers. Rescuer/enabler relationships are possible; share your dreams instead.

Pisces to Libra

You have strong aesthetic inclinations in this location and could become more physically attractive. Here, you prefer harmony and ease, and are susceptible to taking the easy way out, as well as being in love with love and overly romantic. You are likely to attract people who know what they want and seem tougher than you are, and you can adopt almost any persona to please people.

Pisces to Scorpio

Intuition is strong and emotions are accentuated, but much is likely to be kept inside and hidden from others. Intimacy may be idealized, and expectations could be very high. Gut reactions are the most accurate. If you're shy, you can develop a more forceful persona. Practical matters are emphasized in relationships, and comfort and money are priorities.

Pisces to Sagittarius

Utopian ideals are probable; seeking the best is a strong urge. Expectations may be higher than can be reached (for yourself and/or others), and some tension is likely as you struggle with being truthful or telling "little white lies" to keep from hurting people's feelings. Action is directed toward seeking the ultimate answers to life, and intellectual stimulation is emphasized in relationships.

Pisces to Capricorn

The dreamer side of you comes down to earth and gets to work in this location, where you find practical ways to use imagination, mystical inclinations, or visionary potentials. Your emotional nature becomes tempered by common sense and the bottom line, and the desire to achieve increases. Caretaking and support (who does what for whom) are central issues in relationships.

Pisces to Aquarius

Compassion is directed toward the wider world, and ideals and humanitarian instincts are accentuated. A revolutionary approach to spiritual matters is possible. Logic and intuition can be effectively combined, and your conscious and unconscious minds work well together. You want more excitement in your relationships and could be drawn to dramatic, larger-than-life individuals.

6
Changing Midheaven Signs

The Midheaven (tenth-house cusp) is associated with career, status, achievement, and fame. As the highest point in the chart, it also represents recognition, honors, and reputation. Of course, the Midheaven also can bring the opposite, such as a corporate CEO accused of fraud.

For most people, the Midheaven represents career (versus job, which is more a sixth-house matter)—the field that represents your life's work.

The point opposite the Midheaven is the IC (fourth-house cusp), which is associated with home and family. It's appropriate that these two major facets of life—career and family—are represented by opposite points in the chart. Managing both successfully is a balancing act.

Here are some broad guidelines to use in interpreting Midheaven sign changes:

- If you want to be a leader in your career, rise to a top position, or make the most of a career in an entertainment-related field, put a fire sign (Aries, Leo, Sagittarius) on the Midheaven.

- If you want steady (but not necessarily speedy) progress in attaining your career goals, material success, or a promising outlet for your practical skills, put an earth sign (Taurus, Virgo, Capricorn) on the Midheaven.

- If you want a career in communications, technology, or a field that requires strong people skills, put an air sign (Gemini, Libra, Aquarius) on the Midheaven.
- If you want a career that would benefit from empathy, nurturing skills, or the ability to delve into the depths (on a conscious, practical, or subconscious level), put a water sign (Cancer, Scorpio, Pisces) on the Midheaven.

Before reading on, identify the Midheaven sign in your birth chart. Do the same with your favorite locations, those under consideration for relocation, and anywhere you spent a significant amount of time during your childhood and teen years.

If you're interested in a specific career, look through the following lists to find the sign associated with it. Here are some general possibilities.

Career Possibilities for Each Midheaven Sign

Aries Midheaven

Working on your own (entrepreneur or solo operator); working outdoors; working with metal tools and weapons (dentist, surgeon, butcher, etc.); careers that involve men or the military; vocations that require much energy and movement (stunt person, ranger, physical education teacher, fire fighter, construction worker, etc.); highly competitive fields; sports; anything involving speed (e.g., race car driver).

Taurus Midheaven

Working with the earth (farmer, rancher, etc.), in financial fields (from cashier to economist to investment adviser, treasurer, etc.), providing material goods and goodies (particularly luxury items such as gourmet foods); sensually satisfying careers; physical manipulation (e.g., chiropractic); working just for a paycheck; vocations that emphasize tactile forms of beauty (sculpture, jewelry designer, flower grower, arranger, or seller, etc.) and singing; fields highlighting sugar (e.g., candy maker).

Gemini Midheaven

Media work or anything that involves using the hands, eyes, mind, or tongue (from hairdresser to tennis player to card dealer); two careers at once; teaching, speaking, or fields that allow you to collect and disseminate information; dealing with facts and figures;

transportation; working with the telephone; clerks of all kinds; automobile business or working on the railroad; vocations involved with literature.

Cancer Midheaven

Providing basic commodities (food, shelter, clothing) for people (e.g., hotels, restaurants, and other businesses); working as a professional nurturer (e.g., nanny); working in a family business or from your home; sharing a career with a family member; providing protection to others; serving the homeland (various patriotic endeavors); nurturing people, pets, or plants; working in fields involving women, liquid, the sea, land, or real estate.

Leo Midheaven

Working in the entertainment world, sales, or promotion; teaching; advertising, drama; stage work; anything accenting creativity or self-expressive acts; working with children or loved ones; fields involving romance, gambling, or speculation, or anything that allows you to be a star; stockbroker; working in the toy business or any kind of recreation, including casinos and cruise lines; trainer or coach or motivational speaker; working literally with felines or gold.

Virgo Midheaven

Health and healing fields, including medicine, physiotherapy, nutrition, herbs, etc.; repairs; efficiency expert; problem-solving; organizing; dealing with facts and figures; technical work; research; anything that requires skill with details or analysis and careful discrimination; fields involving much paperwork or communication (linguist, clerk, author, announcer); cleaners of all sorts; repair people (fixers); fields that require good craftsmanship and/or careful hygiene.

Libra Midheaven

Fields involving beauty or balance; vocations in which your personal grace, charm, or diplomatic skills are assets; artistic vocations (particularly the visual arts, such as graphic design, architecture, photography, or fashion); counselors and consultants of all kinds; therapists; having a business partner or working with a marital partner; providing adornment or decoration for others; catering to people's vanity; marital counselor; wedding planner (or any work that encompasses weddings).

Scorpio Midheaven

Fields that arouse intense emotions or involve life-and-death circumstances (hospice worker; embalmer; etc.); depth psychotherapy; politics; the sex industry; working beneath the surface (mining, pipe fitting, etc.); vocations that include danger or physical abuse (police work, boxing, football, etc.); work that strives to transform people (pharmacist, surgeon, other healing arts); dealing with joint resources (stockbroker, IRS agent, investment counselor, researcher whose funding comes from government grants); garbage and recycling.

Sagittarius Midheaven

Fields that involve education, travel, other countries, other cultures, philosophy, religion, or anything that is inspirational or seeks a higher truth; exploring and adventuring and venturing far afield; idealistic fields (minister, ombudsman, consumer advocate, etc.), wheeler-dealer or big-time promoter; journalist, judge, lawyer, or anyone concerned with the pursuit of justice; someone who wields more influence than the average worker; working literally with horses, fat, abundance, endowments, or large animals.

Capricorn Midheaven

Being in charge (boss, executive, president); any and all business fields or vocations requiring common sense and pragmatism; earth-related fields (such as geology or gems); fields requiring specialized training (such as vocational schooling or graduate school) or that are highly structured; working literally with older people, teeth, minerals, bones, salt, or time.

Aquarius Midheaven

Working in a field that is unusual or unconventional (including astrology); group activities (such as a group practice); representing others (e.g., state legislator); fields involving new technology or anything futuristic; humanitarian work or social activism; New Age pursuits; work that is part-time or erratic or has unusual hours or nonstandard conditions; self-employment; working literally with accidents, airlines, clubs, divorce, science fiction, or lightning.

Pisces Midheaven

Fields that are glamorous (e.g., stage and screen) or involve a high degree of imagination or strong visualization skills; compassionate pursuits (medicine, charitable activities, etc.); work that has a strong element of spirituality or religion; identifying underlying patterns (historian, sociologist, scientist, etc.); working with the infinitely large (e.g., astronomer) or the very small (e.g., microbiology); working with clients/customers that are escapist (therapist, suicide intervention, bartender, etc.); using your intuition in your work.

Now find the section below for your natal Midheaven and, within that section, read the information for the relocated Midheaven sign. Remember, both the Midheaven and the IC change signs.

Aries Natal Midheaven

Aries to Taurus

You can develop more staying power workwise as the "I'll do it once and move on" tendency of Aries shifts toward the perseverance and completion of Taurus. Personal will and determination are emphasized, and you know what you want to do and how you want to do it. You may seek a vocation that brings you more pleasure or monetary gain, or you could be drawn to fields involving sensuality, comfort, financial matters, the earth, or luxuries. Diplomatic tendencies in the home environment become more intense and probing; you ferret out secrets and uncover hidden motivations among family members.

Aries to Gemini

Variety is the spice of your vocational life. You thrive on new experiences and new challenges, but are easily bored. Your entrepreneurial instincts may be in fields involving communication, the media, paperwork, teaching, speaking, or any kind of intellectual stimulation. Perhaps your work involves dexterity, eye-mind-hand coordination, transportation, or physical agility. On the home front, tact is waning and honesty (sometimes bluntness!) is taking over.

Aries to Cancer

A pioneering approach shifts toward seeking more security in the vocational realm. Your natural desire for independence could be softened by working with family members or in fields involving home, land, real estate, nurturing, protection, food, shelter, or clothing. Both compassion and competition are highlighted. In regard to domestic matters, equalitarian instincts are replaced by a sense of responsibility and determination to take charge.

Aries to Leo

Go-getting tendencies are accentuated, as are action, initiative, and courage. You crave excitement within your vocation, so boring or ordinary careers would be hard to take. A natural entrepreneur, you want to be a mover-shaker-doer in the world. The rush of adrenaline has strong appeal. You may utilize charisma, dramatic talent, sales ability, promotional skills, creativity, or leadership within your work. Your enthusiasm tends to be contagious, and you get others involved. At home, a more unconventional note enters the mix. Family members may be less predictable; you may shake up the routines within the nest.

Aries to Virgo

A desire for tangible results gains priority within your ambitions. Confidence and initiative remain, but you have more patience and follow-through now. Vocations involving health, healing, efficiency, repairs, paperwork, or any kind of improvement are options. You can analyze well and are apt to spot the flaws (and how to fix them) quickly. On the home front, aesthetics are strongly emphasized. The desire for a smooth, easy flow in the domestic realm is accentuated.

Aries to Libra

Self-directed efforts now shift more toward partnership and teamwork on the job. You may elect to share a career with your beloved, or to work in fields that involve lots of interpersonal interactions, beauty, balance, harmony, diplomacy, or justice. Both at home and at work, you may find a better balance between assertion and accommodation, between personal needs and the desires of others, between going it alone and sharing efforts with others.

Aries to Scorpio

Willpower is accentuated with this combination, and you're ready to take your vocational experience to a deeper level. Where Aries likes to do things once and move on, Scorpio loves to probe the depths, explore the layers, and uncover all the possibilities. You might be drawn to fields that involve emotional intensity, life-and-death situations, taboos, occult studies, hidden matters, joint resources, politics, or anything that involves looking beneath the surface of life. You can spot nuances and read the nonverbal cues around your workplace. On the home front, a preference for ease, comfort, and beauty is emphasized.

Aries to Sagittarius

Your pioneering spirit and eagerness to explore new vocational territory are accentuated. You take risks and try things—often before other people do. Action, movement, and excitement are highlighted. Independence remains a big priority. You may be attracted to fields involving education, enlightenment, travel, other cultures, philosophy, religion, the law, or anything that broadens people's horizons, whether physically, mentally, or spiritually. You can inspire others through your work. In domestic matters, the emphasis is on sharing and communication. A free exchange of ideas and cooperative inclinations are in focus.

Aries to Capricorn

You, the independent operator, are ready to take over and run the show for other people. Doing your own thing is less of a priority than gaining power, mastery, and expertise in the vocational world. Your ambitions are apt to rise, and you're likely to seek more authority and power. You may confront some authority figures—or some practical limits—along the way. Fields that involve older people, minerals, time, quality, corporations, or other bureaucracies could be a draw now. You are ready to be reliable, responsible, and realistic. Domestic matters emphasize a parenting motif. Protective instincts are highlighted, along with warmth and family feelings.

Aries to Aquarius

You can be the rebel in your career, breaking the rules or stepping outside the boundaries in your quest for achievement. You might be drawn to vocations that involve progress, New Age ideas, new technology, groups, organizations, invention, or anything that is unconventional. You could be good at brainstorming on the job, and may want unusual circumstances, working hours, or conditions. Independence of thinking and action are highlighted. Domestically, the focus is on warmth and love, with a quest for extra excitement and entertainment at home.

Aries to Pisces

You can bring more intuition and imagination into your vocational world, and visualization skills are apt to sharpen. You may be drawn to fields that involve beauty, mysticism, healing, compassion, or imagery, and you're likely to have high standards for your work and yourself as a worker. Your inner world becomes more important; you are not so quick to move into action. (Dreaming takes over from doing.) On the home front, a more pragmatic, "fix-it" focus prevails. The emphasis is on getting the job done, and you and loved ones must be careful to keep a critical attitude directed toward the physical world and not toward one another.

Taurus Natal Midheaven

Taurus to Aries

You're likely to take more initiative in the vocational realm. Where you've been laid-back, you're now more assertive and eager to break new ground. Doing things your way matters much; entrepreneurial and solo ventures have high appeal. You might get more involved with fields that involve men, machines, the outdoors, sports, the military, or anything that is energetic or self-directed. This combination is excellent for being able to start and finish projects. On the home front, a softer, gentler motif moves in. An aesthetically pleasing domicile could become a higher priority.

Taurus to Gemini

Variety moves up on the priority list vocationally. You are eager for intellectual stimulation and lots of different experiences in your professional life, and may get more involved with fields that involve the media, communication, information, dexterity, flexibility, or eye-mind-hand coordination. You could juggle two careers at once, and you can put people at ease in the workplace. On the home front, the urge for expansion could hit. You might want to enlarge your home, travel more, or bring in more inspirational activities (e.g., philosophy, religion, education, etc.).

Taurus to Cancer

Safety and stability remain significant vocational goals; you want a career that is dependable. You might work with family members or in fields involving land, real estate, food, shelter, clothing, or other basic commodities. Sticking to the status quo is likely. On the home front, issues of power and control are in high focus. This could manifest as power struggles with loved ones or interactions that feature strong willpower and decided opinions. Being able to equitably share responsibilities is a major issue.

Taurus to Leo

You're ready to risk for greater gain as your former orientation toward comfort and stability morphs into a desire for drama, excitement, and bigger and better things in the vocational realm. You want to be a leader, to gain recognition and applause from others. You could become more involved in fields involving children, romance, entertainment, sales or promotion, teaching, speculation, or anything that allows you to be center stage. You might work with loved ones. A bit more detachment is likely on the home front. Logic and an objective eye move in to replace the intensity that was present before. Personal will is accentuated.

Taurus to Virgo

You could end up working harder than ever before because getting results and doing things well matters so much to you. You may be drawn to fields that involve health, nutrition, healing, repairs, paperwork, facts, figures, analysis, technical matters, or any kind of improvement. Your efficiency quotient is high, and you can be quite organized, thorough, and effective. On the domestic front, sensitivity, emotions, and unconscious reactions are featured. High ideals about your home (and/or loved ones) are likely, and you may be motivated to make your domicile more attractive.

Taurus to Libra

You have the potential to enjoy your work, especially to find pleasure in teamwork and cooperating with others. People-oriented fields are likely, although aesthetic pursuits are another option. You are likely to sharpen skills used to compare and contrast, to weigh and balance different options. You may work with a partner. Diplomatic skills could prove valuable on the job. Regarding domestic matters, the movement is toward more action and independence within the home and by family members.

Taurus to Scorpio

Financial fields are favored. You may be able to use money to make money or earn royalties or other forms of delayed income. Feelings about your career become more intense as you leave behind a laid-back attitude and are drawn to fields that provoke strong emotional reactions in you. This could include exploring occult studies, taboo topics, hidden matters, detective work or research, life-and-death confrontations, psychotherapy, manipulations (politics, physiotherapy, acupressure, chiropractic, etc.), or anything that looks beneath the surface. In the domestic realm, you'll be a bit more easygoing and oriented toward comfort. Sensual indulgence is a priority.

Taurus to Sagittarius

Idealism moves up on the vocational priority list as financial recompense moves down. You still want to be paid well for your labors, but you're more focused on your professional dreams and visions. You're eager to conquer new worlds and expand your horizons, and may be drawn to work that involves education, enlightenment, philosophy, travel, metaphysics, or anything that broadens people's perspectives. You want to do more than you have done before! On the home front, an intense, emotional focus shifts toward a love of variety, restlessness, and quest for more information.

Taurus to Capricorn

Dependability, reliability, and endurance are accentuated, and you can do well in any business field or wherever steady, regular routines are involved. You can be quite dedicated, thorough, organized, and persistent. You're ready to take charge of your work life and will seek avenues to hone your expertise and become an authority figure in your career. Emotions, money and assets, and issues of dependency and unconscious inclinations are in focus in the domestic realm.

Taurus to Aquarius

Your desire for comfort, good financial remuneration, and stability in a career shifts toward an emphasis on independence, inventiveness, and a love of variety and change. You're willing to take risks to get more stimulation and intellectual understanding. You may work outside the Establishment or in fields that are progressive, New Age, unusual, or involve unconventional approaches or hours. Domestic concerns emphasize strong will, determination, and a quest for excitement and stimulation.

Taurus to Pisces

The desire for a smooth, easy flow on the job is accentuated. You want a comfortable situation in which people do *not* rock the boat; you also might play the role of appeaser or peacemaker. However, you could go too far to avoid discomfort. Your work might involve creative imagination, healing, intuition, visualization skills, beauty, or compassion. Domestically, the accent is on practicality and doing a good job. Some criticism or flaw-finding could occur; try to direct it toward the material world rather than at people.

Gemini Natal Midheaven

Gemini to Aries

You want more independence and self-direction in your work, and your vocational confidence could rise. Fields that involve the outdoors, men, military, metal tools and weapons, being a pioneer, or operating on your own are favored. In this location you're more easily bored, preferring to do things once and move on. You could be more competitive on the job now. On the home front, the desire for teamwork increases, and beautifying your domestic environment is likely to be a higher priority.

Gemini to Taurus

You probably want more vocational stability and security. No longer content to multitask and pursue many different interests, you're drawn to fields that promise dependability, good pay, and comfortable conditions. You want to enjoy your work and could labor in fields that indulge others or involve finances, the earth, or material goods. Emotions are likely to be more intense in the home, where unconscious crosscurrents are possible. Pay attention to the vibes and nonverbal cues.

Gemini to Cancer

Versatility and multiple interests shift toward the goal of security and safety. Your natural communication skills could be directed toward serving the public, working with family members, or working in fields such as real estate, restaurants, hotels, or anything meeting the basic needs of people. Protection becomes a higher priority. On the domestic front, wanderlust lessens and a desire for control, stability, and regularity increases. Parental motifs are highlighted. Responsibility and reliability are mantras for the domestic realm.

Gemini to Leo

Your versatility and multiple talents are likely to be directed into the world at large because you're ready to sparkle and shine, to be a star in your career. This could involve fields such as entertainment, promotion, creative arts, recreation, etc., or might involve working with children or loved ones. Your sense of humor could be a vocational asset, and an extroverted focus is present, so you can draw people out and get them involved. On the home front, the emphasis is on independence and respecting each person's individuality. An adventurous spirit reigns.

Gemini to Virgo

Mental mastery is the vocational motif for you, and this location accents talent for teaching, collecting and disseminating information, dealing with facts, figures, or paperwork, writing, speaking, technical matters, nutrition, or the healing arts. Although you've probably been scattered and overextended in the past, you're more organized and focused now. Getting tangible results—seeing the fruits of your labors—is important. You want to finish things. On the home front, a sensitive, idealistic motif prevails. Seeing the best in loved ones is likely, although setting standards too high and being disappointed is also possible. Compassion and aesthetic skills are emphasized within the domicile.

Gemini to Libra

You can work very well with people in just about any setting in this location, as strong communication skills are highlighted. You also operate well as a team player and can help others feel comfortable about shared efforts. Here, it's natural for you to bounce ideas back and force and to instinctively try to make sure everyone is heard. Aesthetic abilities may be further developed. You could work with a partner in this locale. On the home front, independence, adventure, action, and movement are highlighted.

Gemini to Scorpio

Although you could have had dual careers in the past, you're sharply focused now, with an intense, laserlike quality. You want to go deeper and deeper into whatever you do. Interest is strong in matters that lie beneath the surface of life, and your curiosity is directed toward life-and-death circumstances, therapy, joint resources, occult studies, or other taboo or intensely emotional arenas. On the domestic front, the focus has moved from exploration and adventure to comfort and stability. You want to consolidate.

Gemini to Sagittarius

This sign combination is one of the natural student, teacher, and traveler; all could be featured in your career. You need lots of stimulation, excitement, and broadened horizons in your work and could easily become bored. Variety is important. (Job-hopping is one danger.) You will drive to do your best and be the best, and might sometimes want more than is possible (dissatisfied with ordinary jobs). Confidence and the willingness to risk for greater gain are accentuated. The home front also features lots of change, new experiences, and intellectual stimulation. Restlessness is a keynote.

Gemini to Capricorn

You, the social butterfly, buckle down and become the executive in the power suit as you move from a love of variety and social exchange to a drive for power and control in the workplace. Ambitions are on the rise. You can be very focused, responsible, and achievement-oriented now, and want to bring your ideas down to earth and make them productive. An informal style becomes more formal and conventional. Domestically, the emphasis shifts from a love of travel, adventure, and fresh ideas to a desire for security, safety, and protection.

Gemini to Aquarius

This combination is very sociable, so you relate well to lots of different people. Communication skills are highlighted, and a love of change and variety is strong. However, boredom is a potential problem, so try to focus on lots of different projects, people, and ideas. A set routine is probably inadvisable. You work well with other people and naturally make friends on the job, where your inventive mind is a vocational asset. On the home front, the emphasis is on fun, excitement, entertainment, lightness, and laughter.

Gemini to Pisces

Settling into one vocational choice is apt to be a challenge. You have multiple talents and high ideals and may yearn for that perfect, "happily ever after" career that does not exist. Choose one (or two) fields to pursue even if they're not as inspirational as you would like. You can excel in healing professions, with beauty or aesthetics, in visualization, or using your communication skills to uplift others or make a better world. You probably can blend logic and intuition well, and flexibility is one of your strengths. Domestically, the emphasis moves from visions and dreams to pragmatism, facing facts, and working hard.

Cancer Natal Midheaven

Cancer to Aries

You're likely to have more confidence and initiative in the vocational realm, where safety and security take second place to independence, initiative, and action. You may gravitate toward fields involving metal tools or weapons, men, the military, the outdoors, sports, or anything self-directed or energetic, and have less patience for repetitive tasks. On the home front, control needs shift toward a teamwork emphasis. Diplomatic skills and aesthetic talents are highlighted in the nest.

Cancer to Taurus

Stability and comfort are priorities in the vocational realm. You will want emotional safety as well as financial security. You may find ways to get more pleasure (or money) from what you do professionally, or you could be drawn to fields involving material possessions, finances, sensual indulgences, the earth, or relaxation and comfort. Domestically, the focus remains pragmatic and dedicated. Working from or in the home is possible. (Family members could also be a part of your career.) Common sense is accentuated.

Cancer to Gemini

Security is less important as you yearn for more variety within your career. You may decide to juggle two vocations in this locale. Your versatility is apt to increase, and you can use multiple talents within the vocational realm, particularly in anything involving communication, information, paperwork, dexterity, transportation, or eye-mind-hand coordination. You can be more objective and lighthearted about professional matters (less emotionally reactive). On the home front, you want more adventure, mental stimulation, and broadened horizons. You may want to travel more or enlarge your nest.

Cancer to Leo

You're ready to have a major impact in your career field! Leadership skills are highlighted, and you can sparkle and shine, bringing applause and admiration from others. You may be drawn to fields in the entertainment world, acting, recreation, creative arts, sales or promotion, or work with children or loved ones. Your natural warmth, caring, and protective instincts will be expressed in a more dramatic, visible fashion. On the home front, predictability becomes less important as you seek more excitement, stimulation, and change.

Cancer to Virgo

This combination is that of an excellent caretaker, who looks after and supports people both emotionally and through practical actions. Efficiency is on the rise, and you could get involved with fields such as nutrition, healing, repairs, paperwork, science, writing, or anything dealing with analysis, research, or facts and figures. You're inclined to work harder than ever and might have trouble delegating tasks (tending to feel that you must do it yourself if you want it done right). Capability and compassion are combined. In the domestic realm, the emphasis is on strong feelings, sensitivity, and the desire for a sanctuary—a lovely, serene place that allows you to retreat from the world.

Cancer to Libra

Emotional connections are a priority in your working world, which might include a family member or partner. You might meet a partner through your career, and finding a happy balance between love and work is a major issue for you. Cooperative ventures have more appeal; you enjoy teamwork. You may utilize diplomatic skills, artistic ability, or grace and charm within your profession. Within the nest, the focus moves from control and predictability to independence and spontaneity.

Cancer to Scorpio

You're well attuned to people's feelings and nonverbal cues and can sense hidden agendas and recognize manipulative moves and backroom maneuvers. Intuition is thus a valuable resource within your profession. Skills in research, occult studies, hidden matters, joint resources, and fields that are emotionally intense and demanding are on the upswing. You need some private time to be most efficient, so find a space and make a place to call your own at home. A preference for stability and established routines is indicated on the domestic front.

Cancer to Sagittarius

You're ready to take some risks in the vocational arena, so fulfill your desire to go for the gusto and do something bigger and better. Security takes a back seat to expanding your options and inspiring others. You could be drawn to fields such as philosophy, religion, education, travel, or anything that broadens people's horizons, and you leave behind the familiar because of an increasing focus on the future and distant places. On the home front, you can be less serious and more lighthearted. Variety and mental stimulation become more important in the nest.

Cancer to Capricorn

You want more power and influence in your career in this locale. Realism and responsibility are on the rise, and you're likely to seek authority and may become a mentor to others. The family focus is less strong now, although you might still work with family members or out of your home. Security is a major goal. You want your vocational life to be stable. You're willing to work very hard now to elevate your status. In domestic matters, an increased focus on sharing and caring interactions within the nest is likely. Warm, cuddly feelings are featured at home.

Cancer to Aquarius

You're broadening your perspective in the professional world, and your family focus is enlarged in some way to include humanity or the wider world. The past is less of a draw;

interest in the future increases. You may work with new technology or New Age concepts, or in fields that are unusual. Your inventive skills are highlighted, and independence and variety are highly valued. Power and control are motifs in the domestic arena; you may want to take charge, or family members may become more dynamic (and pushy). A desire for more excitement and entertainment is also likely.

Cancer to Pisces

You're likely to gravitate toward a sheltered environment in your professional life because you want to feel safe and to protect yourself (and perhaps others, as well) from being hurt. A poetic, sensitive, graceful style is likely. You can do well in fields involving creative imagination, healing, inspiration, mysticism, or magic. You may sometimes sacrifice too much in your career, and a desire to make the world better or more beautiful is likely. Within the nest, the emphasized motifs are hard work, common sense, attention to details, health, and cleanliness.

Leo Natal Midheaven

Leo to Aries

Action and excitement are highlighted. You continue to emphasize movement in your professional life, so lots of variety and stimulation are important. Increased independence is possible. You're willing to take on the role of solo operator more often, and find satisfaction in pioneering and being first—leading the way for others. Your natural charisma and promotional skills are oriented toward activities that allow you to do things your way. In the domestic sphere, the emphasis is on communication, teamwork, and friendly interactions. You may elect to beautify your home or spend more time with loved ones.

Leo to Taurus

An increased desire for stability and comfort on the job is likely, and you may look for ways to earn more money, or have a more relaxed work setting. Your natural charisma and dramatic talents remain, but you're more interested in what is established and reliable. (Risk-taking moves down the priority list.) Your endurance and dedication are excellent. On the home front, strong wills are highlighted. A casual, individualistic focus shifts toward more emotional intensity and a tendency to delve deeply into issues.

Leo to Gemini

Your versatility is enhanced in this locale, where your natural creativity and charisma flow easily into communication, commerce, transportation, dexterity, paperwork, writing, speaking, or collecting and disseminating information. You can be an excellent teacher, coach, or trainer. A sense of humor is a likely vocational asset, and you bring a dynamic, dramatic element to any discussion. In domestic matters, the emphasis is on independence, the urge to explore, and a desire for mental stimulation.

Leo to Cancer

You're likely to take fewer risks, and being center stage is less important here than is an established, secure professional base. You want professional safety. You may gravitate toward fields involving land, real estate, nurturing, protection, food, clothing, shelter, etc., and may work with family members. Your demeanor is warm and supportive. In your nest, the motif moves from an unconventional, freedom-loving focus to a cautious, careful, responsible one. Doing the right thing matters much.

Leo to Virgo

You're likely to work harder here, where tangible results have a high priority. You may enhance your talent for medicine, nutrition, science or technical fields, repairs, or anything that allows you to fix flaws or enhance the efficiency of a project. You no longer have to be the star in your field; working humbly behind the scenes is okay. Your natural fire and confidence are now backed up by stamina and finishing power, so you can accomplish much. In domestic matters, the motifs are transpersonal, interest in the wider world, and a blend of logic and intuition.

Leo to Libra

Relationships move up on the priority list, and you might work with a partner or in people-oriented fields. You can be quite charming, magnetic, sociable, and attractive, able to both lead and cooperate effectively with a team. Creative and artistic pursuits are favored. On the home front, independence and adventure are highlighted. Family members are apt to go their own way, and you're likely to be active and eager to try new things.

Leo to Scorpio

Issues of control and power are in focus, and your willpower is quite strong. You're at your best running the show. Capable of tremendous endurance, loyalty, and determination, you excel in fields involving joint resources, investigation, life-and-death matters, or intense emotions. You easily dig up hidden information and sense what people are thinking and feeling but not saying. You can do well in office politics. In your nest, the emphasis is on a fixity of purpose, desire for comfort, and quest for increased sensual satisfaction.

Leo to Sagittarius

This combination is fiery and exciting. You're eager and full of vitality, ready to do bigger and better at all times. An expansive tendency is present, and you want to enlarge your professional scope. Talent as a teacher, promoter, persuader, or coach is likely; you can inspire others and encourage them to be all that they can. You could develop more interest in travel, education, enlightenment, or seeking higher truth in your career. The motifs highlighted for home and family are communication, objectivity, and multiple interests. Variety and diversity are important.

Leo to Capricorn

You want to be in charge, and have more patience now and the desire to work your way to the top. Leadership skills and ambition are accented. Your natural sparkle is backed by perseverance, dedication, and a willingness to work hard; you can get the job done very well. Your charisma can be quite effective in the business world, or in fields of entertainment, recreation, or the creative arts. On the home front, a cool, collected focus shifts to emotional warmth, caring, and commitment. Security within the nest is a higher priority.

Leo to Aquarius

Being the star is less important now; you're willing to be a part of a cooperative group. Passions and excitement are still high, but you can balance that with objectivity and a detached perspective. You may be drawn to fields involving new technology, progress, humanitarian ideals, or anything that is unusual or unconventional. Your networking skills are highlighted. In the domestic realm, the emphasis is on finding a happy medium between the heart and the head and between an urge to be special versus a desire to share equally with others. Excitement comes more easily. Things get stirred up.

Leo to Pisces

Magic is in the air. Your visualization skills are accentuated, and you may gravitate toward professions involving beauty, compassion, or the creative imagination. You can be quite persuasive and magnetic, swaying people to see things your way. But, an idealistic quest for the "perfect job" could lead to disappointment or martyrdom. You excel at activities that bring more grace or beauty into the world or assist the less fortunate. On the home front, the emphasis moves from freedom and individuality to an organized focus, practicality, and a willingness to put in sweat equity.

Virgo Natal Midheaven

Virgo to Aries

You're likely to be more confident and independent in your vocational life here, but may become easily bored and need more movement and variety. You may decide to start your own business or seek opportunities to be on your own careerwise. Your profession might involve more contact with men, metal tools and weapons, the outdoors, or assertive action. On the home front, you want a smooth, easy flow. Attractive surroundings are important, and you and family members are likely to try to glide around possible unpleasantness, to minimize disagreements.

Virgo to Taurus

Practical matters are highlighted. You continue to be dependable and steadfast in your professional life, but you may give a higher priority to getting paid well for your labors or to enjoying your work. A flaw-finding focus shifts toward the pursuit of comfort and pleasure in the professional realm. Talent is likely in the business world or in any field that benefits from common sense. In the domestic realm, you're sensitive and intuitive. Family members are apt to keep some things to themselves, to reveal little. You may have to dig to get to the bottom of family-related issues.

Virgo to Gemini

Now that you've focused on quality in your profession, you're ready to pursue quantity. A careful, precise, analytical focus shifts toward a love of variety and interest in myriad areas. Talent is particularly likely in fields involving thinking, communication, writing, paperwork, transportation, media, or the gathering or disseminating of information. It's easier to scatter your forces here, so clear priorities are essential. Idealism is highlighted in the domestic realm. High expectations are likely on the part of family members (perhaps too high). Sharing inspirational activities is a better choice than looking to someone else to create a "heaven on earth" feeling.

Virgo to Cancer

You're likely to be a natural caretaker and could make a career out of looking after other people. You also might work with family members, or just be a "mother of the world" type. Compassion and competence are blended. You can attend to people's emotional and physical needs, and be successful in both arenas. You may be drawn to fields that allow you to nurture others, to heal them, or to enhance their lives. On the home front, a desire for more control and predictability is likely. What was vague before is now brought into sharp focus.

Virgo to Leo

You're ready to take the lead, to get some recognition for your skills. No longer the humble servant laboring behind the scenes, you're ready to shine, to be a star, to display your charisma in the professional realm. You can promote yourself careerwise and may receive more positive attention or recognition from the world. Your natural efficiency is backed up with dynamism and enthusiasm, so you accomplish a great deal. Regarding home and family, a soft, gentle motif shifts toward more independence and individuality.

Virgo to Libra

Relationships move up on the priority list as love starts to take precedence over work demands. You might also share a career with a romantic (or other) partner. Your critical, discriminating eye is softened by the ability to be kind and diplomatic, and you can encourage people to improve without hurting their feelings. Craftsmanship is accentuated; you can create items that are both beautiful and functional. What you do or make now is less significant than how the people around you feel, and making positive connections matters much to you. On the home front, the desire for a sanctuary and domestic retreat shifts toward a drive for more excitement and independence.

Virgo to Scorpio

Dedication and commitment are highlighted. You're very motivated to get the job done and to do it well. Organizational skills are accentuated, and you can excel in the business, financial, or research world, dealing well with details and bringing order out of chaos. You may decide to eliminate certain aspects of your vocation or do a major clearing out by getting rid of papers, inefficient procedures, negative habit patterns, etc., in order to make room for something better. Regarding home and family, the accent is on comfortable, easygoing, relaxed interactions. Affection is highlighted.

Virgo to Sagittarius

You're ready for more adventures in your vocation and may enlarge your professional scope or seek out new territory to explore. You could be drawn to fields such as law, education, travel, metaphysics, or anything that uplifts people or connects them with a higher truth. You probably have less patience now and may have very high expectations (for yourself and others). Keep your goals reasonable, and give everyone time to get there. In the domestic arena, the emphasis is on variety, versatility, and visionary perspectives, and a more lighthearted motif is present.

Virgo to Capricorn

Hard work is still on the docket, and a nose-to-the-grindstone approach is likely within your profession. Dedication, discipline, and determination to excel are probable. Self-critical tendencies could be accentuated; don't be too hard on yourself. You'll be dealing personally with authority figures, limits, and boundaries. Don't restrict yourself, but be sensible about what is possible; then you can achieve a great deal. Ignore reality and you could feel frustrated and inhibited. Within the nest, motifs of compassion, sensitivity, and protection are emphasized.

Virgo to Aquarius

Your linear, practical, step-by-step focus shifts toward a broader perspective and the possibility of sudden flashes of insight. You might leap from A to Z without going through all the steps in between. You can bring more inventiveness and innovation into your career, or create chaos out of order. An unconventional attitude may serve you well professionally. You excel at rational analysis and scientific thinking and are probably good at solving problems. On the home front, a gentle, retiring, shy motif morphs into a drive for drama and excitement.

Virgo to Pisces

This combination highlights the polarity between idealism and realism, and is an advantage if you're an artist or craftsperson or are pursuing a career in a healing profession. You can bring visions into form in the material world by manifesting your dreams (and those of others). On the down side, procrastination and perfectionism (never being satisfied) are dangers. On the positive side, you are creating a better or more beautiful world. The shift is toward more dreaming in the workplace and more doing (efficiency) in the domestic realm.

Libra Natal Midheaven

Libra to Aries

The self/other polarity is highlighted for you professionally as a past focus on relationships and people-oriented work shifts toward a desire for more independence and an entrepreneurial spirit. You want to do things your way! You don't lose your talent for teamwork, but are more eager to strike out on your own. You're likely to seek more adventure and movement in your professional life. In the domestic realm, personal will wanes and the desire to share and cooperate increases.

Libra to Taurus

Pleasure is highlighted regarding your professional life. You may work in a field involving beauty or pampering people, or get lots of gratification from what you do, or seek greater financial rewards. You prefer circumstances that are comfortable, where a relaxed, easygoing style is an asset. You know how to soothe people. On the home front, a strong-willed focus is present. Achieving compromises could be challenging. A direct, open style shifts toward more secretive, covert interactions.

Libra to Gemini

You're likely to excel at professional communication, and people skills are accentuated. You can be quite appealing and sociable with others, and do well in any field involving interpersonal interactions, media, or information. Bouncing ideas back and forth with

others is quite natural. You need a lot of mental and social stimulation, and tend to relate to everyone as an equal and encourage sharing and cross-fertilization of concepts.
Within the nest, the focus is on a desire for movement, adventure, and excitement. You
may elect to travel more or enlarge your home.

Libra to Cancer

Protective instincts are triggered. You may seek more professional security and might
work more with family members. A talent for teamwork remains, but you'll be more
concerned with making sure that your position is safe in workplace interchanges. With
this combination, you can probably be swayed by the people in your environment, so
strive to stay centered. Regarding home and family, the shift is from independence and
lots of activity to control, predictability, and doing the right thing.

Libra to Leo

Your confidence quotient is on the rise. You'll be more aware of your leadership skills
and ability to persuade others. Sales and promotional work is favored. In this location
you can be a natural entertainer, and people are likely to be drawn to you. Artistic creativity is another possible talent. You do well at encouraging others and helping them
focus on the positive. You're likely to seek more professional recognition and applause.
On the home front, the emphasis is on personal freedom, individuality, and openness.

Libra to Virgo

You probably put in more sweat equity in this area, as the laid-back (sometimes lazy)
Libra shifts to hard-working, dedicated Virgo. Work for its own sake is more of a priority. Although relationships are still a concern, getting the results you want is now
weighed equally with pleasing the people involved in your projects. Analytical skills are
likely to increase. You become more productive and efficient. In domestic matters, a
forceful, independent motif shifts toward softness, compassion, and empathy.

Libra to Scorpio

You're ready to look more deeply into your professional life and less inclined to accept
first appearances. You dig, probe, and seek to uncover what is hidden. A knack for reading nonverbal cues and sensing hidden agendas is likely. You can excel at politics, ther-

apy, and strategy. Your competitive spirit is apt to increase, along with possible financial or business skills. In terms of the nest, an active, independent motif shifts toward a drive for comfort and stability.

Libra to Sagittarius

You may want to expand your professional possibilities, as a drive to do more than you have done before is likely. Your passion for truth and justice is apt to intensify. Although you could be quite diplomatic before, you're inclined to be very open and honest (perhaps even blunt) in this locale. You can inspire people and help them expand their viewpoints and see greater possibilities. Domestically, a restless motif is still present. You and family members will be drawn to lots of variety and new experiences.

Libra to Capricorn

Here, your executive side takes over from the team player as you seek more influence and power in your professional life. You could feel torn between taking charge versus relating as an equal (treating people as peers). Achievement probably becomes a higher priority than harmonious relationships with colleagues, and you may seek out a mentor or become a mentor to a younger individual. Domestic motifs are apt to shift from independence, action, and movement to emotional connections, safety, and security.

Libra to Aquarius

Your interpersonal and intellectual skills are highlighted. You could become more inventive in this locale, and may want more variety or change in your routines. You can probably make friends with just about anyone in the workaday world. Your objectivity and sense of fairness are valued by people who work with you. On the home front, the themes are lively and exciting, with an extra dose of drama.

Libra to Pisces

Skill with beauty and aesthetics is highlighted, and you may be graceful and charming in your manner or create a lovely environment in which to work. You could excel at any number of artistic pursuits. You're apt to want to please others and might be too accommodating, too inclined to "go with the flow" rather than stand up for yourself. Strong empathy helps you identify what people want. In domestic matters, the emphasis shifts from action and adventure to dedication, craftsmanship, and doing things well.

Scorpio Natal Midheaven

Scorpio to Aries

You're eager to break out on your own. More independence is a strong draw, and direct, open action has greater appeal than indirect routes now. Although you retain your natal perseverance and follow-through, you'll want more movement, variety, and new experiences in this locale. Impatience could increase. Your willpower is emphasized. On the home front, the focus is on pleasure, relaxation, and a comfortable give-and-take with loved ones.

Scorpio to Taurus

Financial skills could be a professional asset, and you might use money to make money. You also can excel at providing comfort or pleasure, and business acumen is likely. Loyalty and follow-through are highlighted. You're apt to be more relaxed and easygoing about your career, and less intense and obsessive. In this location you want to be paid better or to find more gratification in what you do. In the domestic realm, questions focus on how you and loved ones share power, possessions, and pleasures. Beware of swings between overindulgence and too much self-denial. Moderation is the goal.

Scorpio to Gemini

Here, your intense, obsessive professional side transforms into a social butterfly. (Well, not entirely.) You can be more casual and lighthearted about work matters and less inclined to feel everything is a life-and-death issue. You're apt to be more open, to communicate more, keeping fewer secrets. You can effectively blend logic and intuition. In regard to home and family, the emphasis is on action, excitement, and the desire for adventures and broadened horizons.

Scorpio to Cancer

Protective instincts are in high gear, and you want to look after others as well as ensure that your position is secure. You are quite aware of nonverbal cues and the "vibes" and feelings that lie just beneath the surface, sensitive to hidden messages. You may work more with family members or in a nurturing or safeguarding capacity. Dependability and reliability are highlighted on the home front, where property and home ownership become more important.

Scorpio to Leo

Your intense, internal, driven style becomes more open and dramatic (perhaps even flamboyant). You are ready to make a splash, to be noticed and noteworthy in your profession. You may work with loved ones, children, or creative expression. Your confidence is likely to rise, and leadership skills are accentuated. You stand out now. In the domestic realm, the motif shifts from comfortable stability to exciting new experiences and experimentation.

Scorpio to Virgo

Competence rises to a high level. If it's worth doing, you feel it's worth doing well. Organizational skills are accentuated, and you're determined to get tangible results. You can excel in the business world or as an efficiency expert who enhances and improves all sorts of circumstances and projects. A dedication to excellence is highlighted. On the home front, an easygoing, relaxed, private motif is present.

Scorpio to Libra

A probing, suspicious style that looks for hidden messages morphs into a diplomatic, people-pleasing persona on the job. You can charm others. Careers that involve interpersonal relationships are favored, and you may enjoy an element of competition as well. Working with a partner (business or marital) is possible. You may bring more beauty or balance into your vocation. In terms of domestic motifs, the focus shifts from predictable comfort to exciting action (and independence).

Scorpio to Sagittarius

An inward, self-controlled, somewhat secretive professional approach shifts toward honesty, a quest for adventure, and a willingness to take risks for greater gain. You may expand your vocational horizons. Capable of both breadth and depth, you bring much to your career. Extroversion is easier in the workplace. On the home front, the priority shifts from comfort toward variety and multiple interests and activities.

Scorpio to Capricorn

Business skills are probable; financial acumen is likely. You can dig out hidden information and put it to practical use in the world. You want to be in charge, to work your way to the top of the vocational heap, while bringing order out of chaos and handling many demands. Reliability and responsibility are accentuated. You use both intuition (nonverbal cues from others) and common sense in your decision-making. Regarding home and family, the focus is on comfort, safety, and cuddly experiences.

Scorpio to Aquarius

With this sign combination, the obsessive-compulsive worker bee becomes the revolutionary (or, at least breaks loose and breaks free). You want more stimulation, change, and variety in your professional life, and can be more cool and detached (less emotionally intense) about career concerns. You still have plenty of perseverance, but will venture into new territory and exercise your inner genius in inventive ways. The future beckons alluringly. In domestic matters, a push/pull between security and risk-taking is likely. The movement is toward more drama and excitement within the nest.

Scorpio to Pisces

You're attuned to hidden matters in your work and can sense what people are feeling (but not saying) and identify covert agendas and manipulative moves. You're also likely to become even more sensitive and empathic about what is going on around you in the workplace. Visualization skills are stronger. High standards are likely, but don't demand more than is humanly possible (of yourself or others). In the realm of home and family, the focus is on common sense, stability, and pragmatism.

Sagittarius Natal Midheaven

Sagittarius to Aries

Adventure and excitement remain strong lures in your vocational life. You'll want to do things your way and may decide to start your own business; entrepreneurial ventures are appealing. (Close supervision is anathema to you.) Variety and movement attract you and fuel your desires, and personal independence is paramount. On the home front, the emphasis is on communication and equal exchanges with family members.

Sagittarius to Taurus

You shift from a willingness to take vocational risks to wanting comfort and stability. The amount you're paid could become more important, and you want to enjoy your career and get considerable gratification, either from what you do or in terms of financial rewards. In domestic matters, a lighthearted motif shifts toward intense emotions and a tendency to dig, probe, and find easy, surface answers unacceptable.

Sagittarius to Gemini

Restlessness and a love of variety remain accentuated. You can excel at any field involving teaching, writing, talking, collecting or disseminating information, or working with the media, where your sense of humor could be a vocational asset. Easily bored, you need lots of mental challenges and changes of routine. Travel for business and pleasure is a possibility. The same casual, flexible, intellectually stimulating motifs are present on the domestic front.

Sagittarius to Cancer

Security moves up on the priority list in this location. Where you would take significant risks (hoping for greater gain) in the past, you're now more apt to play it safe. You may work more with a family member or in fields that involve providing basic needs for people, such as food, clothing, and shelter. A more sober note moves in on the home front. The focus is on realism, responsibility, and doing the right thing.

Sagittarius to Leo

The lure of an adrenaline rush remains quite strong, and you continue to need an exciting career, preferably one that allows you the chance to be a star and gain positive attention, applause, and admiration. Promotional and persuasive skills are likely. You can motivate others and get them eager to participate in your projects. You may work more with loved ones or in fields involving recreation, creativity, entertainment, or romance. Domestically, the shift is toward more independence and freedom, but with lots of good ideas bouncing back and forth.

Sagittarius to Virgo

You're apt to focus more on the details now, as your "big picture" vocational view and working style changes to one with more focus and concentration. A step-by-step approach is appealing. Here, your visionary skills can be applied to the everyday world, with good, practical results. Competence and craftsmanship are high on the priority list. On the home front, overextension is likely. You could be pulled in many different directions and have a hard time making (and keeping) clear priorities.

Sagittarius to Libra

You can charm people associated with your career, where your natural magnetism and other attractive qualities are enhanced. You do well with interpersonal interactions and might work more with a partner or spouse. Adventure and excitement within your career takes a back seat to establishing comfortable relationships. Domestically, the accent is on a love of variety and a quest for lots of action, excitement, and self-directed pursuits.

Sagittarius to Scorpio

You are ready to take things to a deeper level. You probe, investigate, and try to get to fundamental, root causes within your vocational life. You may develop better financial skills or do well in research or in understanding nonverbal cues. In the domestic arena, the shift is toward more comfort and stability with less restlessness and need for variety. You settle in and pursue sensually satisfying activities.

Sagittarius to Capricorn

Ambition is on the upswing. Where you've been independent (and perhaps a bit wild) in the past, you're now focused on making your way to the top, earning a position of power and respect. A major plus is your willingness put in extra effort to hone your skills to gain the influence and executive power you desire. Regarding home and family, the focus shifts from flexible and flippant to serious and cautious. Emotional ties become more important to you.

Sagittarius to Aquarius

Having independence within your career remains a major priority. You want to feel free to do your own thing and to experiment with different approaches or even different vocations. Under this adventurous influence, you may discover more ways to break the rules or work outside the Establishment or be involved with transpersonal or humanitarian pursuits. On the domestic front, the emphasis is on laughter, loving, and entertainment. You may sparkle more within the home.

Sagittarius to Pisces

Dreams and visions are highlighted in your professional life. You could do well in aesthetic fields, any arena in which images are important, or where the ability to envision possibilities is a vital skill. You're apt to have high standards for your career (perhaps even wanting more than is possible) and for yourself as a worker. Remember, nobody is perfect! On the domestic front, the key motifs are mental, with an eagerness to learn, share ideas, and pursue knowledge in all its forms.

Capricorn Natal Midheaven

Capricorn to Aries

You may be more confident within your profession. Extra energy and initiative are likely, and you're apt to seek more action and excitement in your vocational life. The urge to do things your way is intensified, and you may push hard against limits you accepted in the past. You probably have less patience but a more pioneering spirit. Caring and sharing are emphasized in the domestic arena. Domestic motifs move more toward partnership, and a desire for equality could become stronger than the tendency to look after others. You may beautify your home.

Capricorn to Taurus

Reliability is still a vocational priority, but you're likely to shift from discipline and hard work toward more comfort, gratification, and financial reward. Feeling good about what you do is a major goal now, as is being well paid for your efforts. You can be more relaxed and have the ability to kick back (while still being very effective). Patience, stability, dependability, and business skills are highlighted. On the home front, the focus is on emotional connections, intuitive understanding, and prizing private space and time.

Capricorn to Gemini

This sign combination is defined as the executive who morphs into the professional dabbler. Here, you're more skilled at multitasking, and may even decide to take on two careers. Your serious, sober approach shifts toward a more lighthearted one, and flexibility, communication skills, and knowing when to "lighten up" serve you well in the working world. In domestic matters, a security focus shifts toward a love of adventure and broadened horizons. You may travel more or fill your home with books, people from other cultures, philosophical discussions, or inspirational activities.

Capricorn to Cancer

You find new ways to blend work and home. This could include a home-based business, working with family members, or gravitating toward a career that involves land, real estate, protection, or providing basic sustenance or support to people. You're likely to find a good balance between spending time and energy on success and making it in the outer world versus spending time and energy with family members and establishing a secure emotional foundation. You can be warm and empathic as well as pragmatic and focused on the bottom line.

Capricorn to Leo

Leadership skills are highlighted, but getting positive attention (and recognition) for your efforts is a higher priority now. You're not only willing to take charge and make things happen, you want to be noticed for doing so. You may receive more renown in this locale, where you can bring in an element of fun or entertainment to hard work. You add confidence and charisma to pragmatism and competence. In domestic matters, security is less of a priority than the urge for new and different experiences. You may make significant changes in the nest and are likely to encourage individuality in family members. Uniqueness is valued.

Capricorn to Virgo

A dedication to excellence continues, and hard work is still in high focus. You can be extremely competent and effective, but this combination can denote a workaholic—taking on too much of the load and not trusting others to help out (or to do things well enough). Learning to delegate could be a challenge. Patience and organizational skills are highlighted, and you do well enhancing or improving situations. Common sense is a vocational asset. On the home front, empathy, compassion, and caring connections are highlighted. Privacy is extra important (having a place to retreat from the world).

Capricorn to Libra

The executive in you becomes more of a team player as you're willing to move from a position of authority to sharing with others. Getting the job done well is still important, but you give equal priority to making people feel good about their accomplishments. Relationships could become more of a focus in your vocation, as could working with a partner or bringing more grace, beauty, or balance into the world. Your charm may prove to be an asset on the job. On the domestic scene, a security focus shifts toward a desire for more action, adventure, and opportunities for each person to do what he or she wants to do.

Capricorn to Scorpio

You can be a natural leader here, directing events with both clear organizational skills and more subtle cues, maneuvering people emotionally. You have a knack for understanding people's needs even when they're not well articulated. Financial skills are probable, business ability is likely, and determination and follow-through are highlighted. You have a good blend of common sense and intuition, and can combine them for optimum results, successfully handling the toughest of tasks. Status is tied less to authority figures (parents) and more to mates and intimate partners. On the home front, the emphasis is on seeking security, comfort, and a relaxed, familiar feeling. Your home should be a haven from the driving and striving that is indicated in the workplace.

Capricorn to Sagittarius

Caution and careful planning morph into an adventurous, exploratory approach, and you're more willing to take risks for greater gain. Your faith, confidence, and optimism are on the rise, so you may venture in where you were afraid to tread in the past. High ideals are indicated. But beware: your expectations (of your career or of yourself as a worker) could become unreasonable and unrealistic. Yet you can see the big picture and are willing to work hard to bring your dreams down to earth. On the home front, safety and familiar routines give way to a desire for variety, mental stimulation, and lots of communication.

Capricorn to Aquarius

Old structures are changing and giving way, and you're now willing to break the rules as a former allegiance to the Establishment shifts toward a more revolutionary style. You can work outside the system now, or re-create the status quo into something totally new. Stability is less of a priority; you take risks and seek excitement, variety, and stimulation. Less set on being in charge, you're more willing to be one of the group, to encourage each person to develop unique perspectives and make a contribution. You're also open to many different alternatives and options. Domestically, the shift is from a desire for warmth, safety, and familiar surroundings to a drive for excitement, drama, and entertainment.

Capricorn to Pisces

A softer, gentler style is likely. You can still take charge, but will be very sensitive and empathic about how you do it. Practical and business skills remain, but you will want to make the world better and more beautiful, or to help or heal in some fashion. Dreams become as important as practical matters. You want an element of inspiration within your career. The ability to visualize will be a vocational asset. In terms of domestic matters, the emphasis is on strong feelings, a desire for privacy, increased intuition, and developing a sheltered, protected environment.

Aquarius Natal Midheaven

Aquarius to Aries

Greater initiative and energy are likely, and self-direction is highlighted; you're eager to call the shots vocationally. Restlessness is probable, so you need lots of different routines and new challenges to avoid boredom. Movement is a plus at work, where you're willing to take risks and venture into fresh territory—a professional pioneer. On the home front, an attractive environment becomes more important. Experiences that are big and dramatic take second place to comfortable, pleasant interactions.

Aquarius to Taurus

Dependability and reliability move higher on the priority list, and your willingness to take vocational risks shifts toward a concern with stability. Predictability has more appeal, including a regular income. You want to enjoy what you do for a living and could tone down some of your natural eccentricity or unconventional attitudes. In this location you probably experiment less, and side with the status quo more often. In domestic matters, the focus is on intense interactions. Strong feelings and much willpower are accentuated within the nest.

Aquarius to Gemini

Communication is emphasized, and your professional life is likely to involve dealing with people and ideas, as well as gathering and managing information. An objective eye is a vocational asset. You may be able to take your work life less seriously, to use humor to help yourself and others "lighten up." Career satisfaction comes through variety, the challenge of new experiences, and continual learning. In terms of family, the emphasis is on excitement, action, and adventure. A lively, enthusiastic mood is indicated within the home.

Aquarius to Cancer

Security becomes increasingly important, so risk-taking is downplayed in this locale. Although you retain an inventive spirit and a willingness to break the rules vocationally, you're more concerned with protecting yourself and others. A safe position has much more appeal. You might also work more with family members or from your home. In regard to the nest, issues of power, mastery, and control are in high focus. Achieving compromises could be challenging. A family that is "all chiefs and no Indians" is possible (everyone wants to run the show).

Aquarius to Leo

In this location you strive to balance several polarities in your professional and domestic lives: being special versus being equal; the head (cool, objective intellect) versus the heart (warm, passionate, expressive); giving priority to friends, groups, or organizations versus loved ones and children. A middle ground is usually best. Leadership skills, charisma, and the ability to motivate others are in high focus. You and family members may be able to master the art of loving without possessiveness—emotional ties that reinforce individuality.

Aquarius to Virgo

You're likely to become more painstaking, thorough, and detail-oriented in your work. In this location a love of variety and stimulation from many different sources shifts toward a desire for tangible results and a need to be practical and grounded in your professional life. Efficiency instincts are highlighted, and you're good at logic, problem-solving, and repairs. In domestic matters, the emphasis changes from excitement, movement, entertainment, and grandstanding toward sensitivity, private time, empathy, and subtle understanding.

Aquarius to Libra

Charm may become one of your professional assets in this location, where you're likely to be more diplomatic and able to please people (although your natural tendency toward independence and unconventionality is still present). Your vocation is apt to feature an emphasis on people and ideas, and you do well as a team player. Your desire for justice and fair play in the workaday world is heightened. On the home front, the trend is toward action, excitement, and independence. You're willing to stir things up to get what you want.

Aquarius to Scorpio

You can probably develop more perseverance in this locale, where follow-through and completion move up in priority; change and variety are not quite as important as before. Emotional interactions begin to become as significant as intellectual connections. You're less detached and more apt to have intense exchanges through your career. In terms of domestic concerns, a shift from excitement toward more comfort and security is likely. You still want to have fun, but are more focused on being able to relax, kick back, and enjoy yourself in the nest.

Aquarius to Sagittarius

The wider world is a likely vocational focus. You can do well in intellectual or New Age careers, or those that expand people's possibilities and choices. A need for independence is heightened. You'll do best on your own, where an adventurous spirit is a likely asset in your career. Variety is important; you need lots of different challenges. Regarding the home front, the emphasis is on a lighthearted, playful attitude and intellectual stimulation. Ideas and conversations probably flow freely between you and family members.

Aquarius to Capricorn

In this location either your rebellious, entrepreneurial self enters the corporate world or your nonconformist side finds a niche. Your unconventional approach to vocational matters is shifting toward more ambition and a desire to be successful within the system. You may bring innovative approaches into the Establishment, or find ways to create a fresh, new structure outside traditional boundaries. You're more willing to take charge now and can be very pragmatic about the bottom line and essential duties. In the domestic realm, warmth and close connections are highlighted. Emotional bonds may be strengthened.

Aquarius to Pisces

You have a wide perspective regarding vocational matters and are oriented toward the greatest good for the greatest number. Bringing in your natural logic and innovative thinking in this location, you now can add intuition and empathy for an effective mix. Your sensitivity and compassion are likely to be directed toward unconventional, progressive, or cutting-edge careers. Idealism is on the rise; don't demand perfection from yourself as a worker. In regard to home and family, the focus is on practicality and efficiency. Fun and games take second place to competence and getting tangible results.

Pisces Natal Midheaven

Pisces to Aries

More confidence is likely in this location, and you could become more assertive in your career or pursue more independence. Although you retain an interest in what is lovely, mystical, imaginative, or inspirational, you want more movement and personal power in this locale. You may break new ground vocationally. On the home front, you could decide to beautify your nest. Criticism shifts toward more diplomatic interchanges.

Pisces to Taurus

Finances move up on the priority list, perhaps surpassing the quest for spiritual or emotional rewards through your work. You are likely to be more stable vocationally, and less apt to be pulled in many different directions. Here, you will want comfort and gratification in the career arena and could develop more patience. You can be tempted by the path of least resistance, and are likely to pursue beauty or harmony in your work. Domestic motifs emphasize an ability to focus and organize, much follow-through, and an attraction to intense emotional interactions.

Pisces to Gemini

Juggling multiple interests is likely to continue to be a challenge, and you may elect to have two (or even more) careers. Talent in a wide array of intellectual and imaginative careers is probable, and objectivity and a lighthearted ability to laugh will help you be less idealistic about your work. You may sharpen your verbal skills. On the home front, a pragmatic emphasis shifts toward a desire for adventure and exploration. You may want to expand your nest or fill it with fascinating ideas and people with a wide array of backgrounds.

Pisces to Cancer

Intuition remains highlighted, and your empathy and ability to tune in to "vibes" on the job is helpful. You may work more with family members. A desire to assist others is emphasized; just be sure you don't do too much, because a "need to be needed" could be carried too far. Vocationally, you're apt to seek more security in this locale. In regard to home and family, the emphasis is on common sense, competence, and responsibly carrying out duties.

Pisces to Leo

You could make more of a splash in this locale, gaining more applause and admiration. What was behind-the-scenes or private is apt to be quite public now, and your confidence could increase, along with an eagerness to take charge (moving away from a "go with the flow" style). Magnetism and persuasive skills are significant vocational talents. In the nest, the desire for freedom is on the upswing. Practical matters take second place to innovation, individuality, and independence.

Pisces to Virgo

Your task in this location is to address the polarity of real versus ideal within your career and in the nest with family members. Negative potentials include procrastination, perfectionism, and chronic dissatisfaction (nothing ever measures up to that internal, ideal standard). The positive side involves bringing a dream into form as an artist, craftsperson, healer, etc. You can envision the most inspiring of possibilities and then work competently to make them manifest in the material world.

Pisces to Libra

A little shelter from the storm is preferred, so you gravitate toward professional situations that allow you to be peaceful and protected. However, the desire to avoid unpleasantness might be overdone. You could work more with a partner or as a team member, and artistic and aesthetic careers are favored, along with people-oriented fields that aid or assist others. In the domestic realm, restlessness is on the rise. A practical focus shifts toward a desire for more movement, adventure, and independence.

Pisces to Scorpio

Emotional control is apt to be a central theme within your career in this location, where the emphasis is on dealing with feelings and gaining mastery over them. You probably will find it easier to stay focused here, your stamina for professional projects could increase, and you can instinctively understand hidden patterns and processes. Regarding home and family, the shift is from hard work and common sense toward comfort, sensual pleasures, and a relaxed attitude.

Pisces to Sagittarius

High hopes are likely, and a talent for inspiration is probable. You'll fare best in fields that involve ideals, beliefs, or values. Restlessness is possible, and perfectionism (wanting the perfect job with the ideal conditions and wonderful colleagues) can result in job-hopping or being let go. You're likely to have greater vocational confidence in this locale and may go for the big time. Curiosity and communication are highlighted in the nest, where the exchange of ideas is important.

Pisces to Capricorn

If your professional style is a bit scattered, diffused, or confused, you can probably concentrate better in this locale, where you can hone your expertise and exercise your leadership muscles. A desire to take charge is likely, and material matters and the bottom line move up on your priority list. A caretaker motif is prominent within the nest. Compassion and competence are blended.

Pisces to Aquarius

You may be more willing to thumb your nose at others concerning vocational matters, thereby moving beyond sensitivity and being easily hurt. Transpersonal careers are favored, and you are drawn to issues involving the wider world and the greatest good for the greatest number. You can be more detached and objective about professional matters in this locale. On the home front, a desire for more fun, frolic, and entertainment is on the rise. Love bonds are accentuated.

7
Planets Changing Houses

As you learned in chapter 1, each of the twelve houses (pie-shaped pieces in the chart) represents certain areas of life, such as romance, career, relationships, money, and communication. When planets change houses in a relocated chart, your emphasis shifts to that area of life. Planets in different houses also give you the opportunity to use your birth chart energy in a different way.

For example, if one or more of your planets move from the natal fifth house to the relocated sixth house, you could use your creativity (fifth house) in your day-to-day work (sixth house). If a planet moves from the relocated first house to the second house (money), you could use your drive and initiative to increase income.

Keep in mind, though, that when one planet changes houses, it's likely that others also do. So, you might benefit from one change but be presented with new challenges with another. Such decisions depend on your mission and goals, your life priorities.

To illustrate: If you have a tendency for wishful thinking, you might want to move to a location that places your Mercury in the relocated third house of communication. But that shift could also, for example, move Uranus into the tenth house, which could trigger sudden career developments—positive or negative.

Here are a few more examples:

One woman was born with a stellium (three or more planets in the same sign) in the relocated fifth house of children, creativity, love affairs, speculation, and drama. She has four children. Her career took off when she moved to an area where the stellium planets were in the sixth house of work (and health).

Another woman was born with a stellium in Taurus, which is oriented toward sensual pleasure, comfort, and ease. Some years ago, a friend persuaded her to visit a sex club in Paris ("just to observe"). In that locale, her Taurus planets are in the relocated eighth house of intimacy, sexuality, joint resources, and intense emotional experiences.

When the chart of another woman is relocated to New York, a city she visits only for business, there are five planets in the tenth house of profession, career, contribution to society, and status, including the Sun and Moon.

A woman who was born with the Sun and Mercury in the watery, inward eighth house became more outgoing and confident when she moved to a location that put the Sun and Mercury in the fiery, extroverted ninth house.

To get an idea of which of your planets change houses when your chart is relocated, calculate your relocated chart (using the CD-ROM) for two or three locations. If you were born in the middle of the country, for example, calculate charts for the East and West Coasts. You'll immediately begin to see the possibilities in each region.

First, however, it's wise to read about the planetary house placements in your birth chart, or the location where you spent the greatest number of childhood or teen years. This will give you a better idea of how the planets in houses operate.

Sun

First-House Sun

With the Sun in your relocated first house, you want more personal recognition and could increase your charisma to be more readily noticed by those around you. Leadership skills might be strengthened, and you could feel more vibrant, alive, excited, and energized.

Second-House Sun

When the Sun is in your relocated second house, you want to make money through creative efforts with loved ones, through risk-taking pursuits, or by taking the lead in any endeavor. You also invest your ego in making money, but can spend outside your budget.

Third-House Sun

Put the Sun in the relocated third house if you want to become more amusing and entertaining. You can sharpen your wits and find more ways to shine by using your mind and communication skills. Persuasive ability could be enhanced, as could public-speaking skills.

Fourth-House Sun

If you want to turn your home into a showplace, put the Sun in your relocated fourth house. This location is also a plus for gaining recognition through family ties, researching your roots or ancestry, or doing something noteworthy or dramatic within your home.

Fifth-House Sun

When the Sun is in your relocated fifth house, you gain more recognition, applause, admiration, or (potentially) fame. Your sense of drama will increase, and you may feel more creative and willing to take risks. Children, romance, or love affairs could become more central to your life.

Sixth-House Sun

When the Sun is in your relocated sixth house, you want to achieve recognition for your competence, efficiency, and ability to fix and repair things or situations. You may take more pride in healthy habits or gain the admiration of others for your common sense and practical skills.

Seventh-House Sun

With the Sun in your relocated seventh house, you want drama and excitement in your relationships and may attract individuals who are larger than life (natural leaders).

Thrill seeking could become significant in your interactions with others. Be cautious if you tend to give away your power to people you admire.

Eighth-House Sun

When the Sun is in your relocated eighth house, you could have a livelier sex life or become more involved with investments and using money to make money. You might take pride in your shrewdness or be noticed for your ability to probe beneath the surface (of life and other people). You may benefit from other people's generosity.

Ninth-House Sun

If you want to become a leader in education, travel, enlightenment, or activities that expand people's horizons, the Sun in your relocated ninth house can help you achieve these goals. You could find lots of thrills in seeking out new countries or fresh experiences, and your charisma quotient could encourage others to go adventuring with you.

Tenth-House Sun

The Sun in your relocated tenth house is a good location if you want to improve your status or gain more recognition in your career. If you want to "go public," this could be the magic placement. Professional promotional efforts are apt to go well, and you may become more influential and important.

Eleventh-House Sun

If you want to meet lots of new people, explore different groups, stimulate progressive thinking, or take pride in being unconventional, the Sun in your relocated eleventh house increases the available opportunities. This placement is also a plus if you want to be a leader in organizations or teamwork.

Twelfth-House Sun

With the Sun in your relocated twelfth house, you could become more involved with creative and artistic pursuits, explore the world of film, be a leader in spiritual or compassionate pursuits, or achieve recognition for your visionary spirit or inspired understanding.

Moon

First-House Moon

With the Moon in your relocated first house, you can learn how to better nurture yourself, as well as focus more on the familial aspects of your life. If you're emotional and sensitive, however, this placement could make you even more so.

Second-House Moon

If you want to hang on to possessions (and money) longer and build pleasurable family connections, put the Moon in your relocated second house. Beware, though, of letting emotions rule your checkbook. Spend wisely.

Third-House Moon

When the Moon is in your relocated third house, you can nurture ideas, spend time on the care and feeding of your mind, integrate emotional and intellectual understanding, and encourage more family discussions.

Fourth-House Moon

If you want to emphasize a strong domestic life, revisit familial feelings from your childhood, strengthen your skills as a caretaker, or deepen the "ties that bind" with those you love, the Moon in your relocated fourth house can help fulfill your desire.

Fifth-House Moon

Children are in focus when the Moon is in your relocated fifth house, as this placement encourages involvement with youth. You may express your creativity within the domestic environment, and be drawn to mutually supportive love relationships.

Sixth-House Moon

If you want to be of service, to assist others, to offer both compassion and competence, the Moon in your relocated sixth house can help you achieve that goal. This placement also promotes common sense, especially if you have strong emotions.

Seventh-House Moon

The Moon in your relocated seventh house is influential if you want to emphasize family involvement, relationships, or establishing partnerships that emphasize mutual caretaking. Caring and sharing with others move up on the priority list.

Eighth-House Moon

With the Moon in your relocated eighth house, you can delve deeply into your own psyche and those of other people. This placement also encourages you to look beneath surface appearances and to explore the connection between nurturing and sexuality.

Ninth-House Moon

If your desire is to fill your home with books, ideas, or people from many different places, or philosophical discussions, the Moon in your relocated ninth house can help you attract what you want. You find security in adventure and in exploring the world.

Tenth-House Moon

When the Moon is in your relocated tenth house, you can solidify your career, play a supportive role on the job, or become more active in vocations involving home, family, land, real estate, the public, women, security, safety, or parenting.

Eleventh-House Moon

If you want to turn family into friends (tolerant, open-minded, accepting) and friends into family (warm, supportive, helpful), the Moon in your relocated eleventh house promotes that desire. You might welcome an unconventional aura or fresh ideas in your home.

Twelfth-House Moon

With the Moon in your relocated twelfth house, you want to create a sanctuary, a private space to get away from it all. Your desire for lovely surroundings is apt to increase, and mystical tendencies may deepen. Nurture spiritual aspirations in yourself and others.

Mercury

First-House Mercury

With Mercury in your relocated first house you can be more spontaneous and quick with your repartee. It's also a plus if you're quiet and reserved and want to strengthen your communication skills and become more open with people.

Second-House Mercury

If you want to make money through your mind or mouth (writing, speaking, sales, media) or through handling information, Mercury in your relocated second house can put you closer to your goal. This placement also favors a pleasant and easygoing communication style.

Third-House Mercury

You're apt to be more verbal and versatile when Mercury is in your relocated third house. Mercury here also can help you become more articulate and multitalented, with a broader range of interests. Your curiosity and lightheartedness could rise.

Fourth-House Mercury

With Mercury in your relocated fourth house, you can improve family communication and bring more mental stimulation into your home through books and gatherings. This placement also might encourage you to learn more about real estate or your roots.

Fifth-House Mercury

Mercury in your relocated fifth house can assist you if you want to become a more dramatic communicator, enhance promotional and persuasive skills (speaking and/or writing), or improve communication with children or loved ones.

Sixth-House Mercury

When Mercury is in your relocated sixth house, you can boost your common sense and enhance communication with colleagues. You also might spend more time thinking about health matters. This is probably not a good placement, however, if you tend to be self-critical.

Seventh-House Mercury

You can enhance communication with partners and others close to you when Mercury is in your relocated seventh house. This placement also can help you develop diplomatic and negotiating skills. You may want to avoid this placement if you quickly tire of relationships.

Eighth-House Mercury

Having Mercury in your relocated eighth house is an advantage if you're doing a major research project for school or work, or an intellectual task that requires much focus and concentration. Here, you also can explore hidden matters and intense emotions.

Ninth-House Mercury

If you're searching for the right school or college location, or want to travel more, explore new ideas, communicate with people from other countries and cultures, or generally broaden your intellectual horizons, Mercury in your relocated ninth house is an asset.

Tenth-House Mercury

Mercury placed in your relocated tenth house can help you become known in your community, seek power through your mind, and better understand authority figures or your parental role. If you're inclined toward guilt or self-criticism, however, choose another location.

Eleventh-House Mercury

With Mercury in your relocated eleventh house, you want more communication with friends and more involvement with organizations, social groups, or causes. This placement also emphasizes stretching your thinking and exploring unconventional ideas.

Twelfth-House Mercury

If you want to write poetry or music, develop your imagination, or explore your compassionate, sensitive side or mystical matters, Mercury in your relocated twelfth house is helpful. If you tend toward "poor me" thinking, however, this is not the place for Mercury.

Venus

First-House Venus

With Venus in the relocated first house, you can add to your physical attractiveness or become more skilled at beauty in action or grace in motion (dancing, skating, gymnastics, tai chi, etc.). You may learn to like yourself better and feel more comfortable with yourself. Sensual pleasures are more important.

Second-House Venus

If you want to attract more from the material world, including money and possessions, Venus in the relocated second house can ease your way. You may generate income through beauty, relationships, or work you enjoy, and comfort is highlighted. You could meet someone special in a bank, where you earn money, or at an arts event.

Third-House Venus

When Venus is in the relocated third house, intellectual pursuits bring pleasure, and you could more fully develop your diplomatic skills. But try not to fall into the trap of saying only what people want to hear. Relationships with siblings may become more loving, and you might meet a partner at a class, in the neighborhood, or through a relative.

Fourth-House Venus

With Venus in the relocated fourth house, you can beautify your home or make your domestic environment more comfortable, lovely, and sensually satisfying. Relationships with parents, children, and other family members may become more affectionate and stable. A domestic activity or relative could connect you with a potential partner.

Fifth-House Venus

If you want more romance in your life, Venus in the relocated fifth house could help you find it. Love affairs could increase in this locale, where your artistic and creative skills may deepen, and love and caring are heightened. Pleasure may come through children and lovers, and you could meet someone at the theater, in the entertainment world, or through a child.

Sixth-House Venus

When Venus is in the relocated sixth house, you can enjoy your work more and be involved in tasks that bring you pleasure. You may develop handicraft skills and make things that are both beautiful and useful. Relationships take on a more practical tone. You might meet a partner at your workplace or through your work.

Seventh-House Venus

With Venus in the relocated seventh house, you're attracted to other people, and one-on-one interactions are apt to increase. Love may be on the horizon. Pleasure is sought and found through relationships, and shared pursuits are most gratifying. You could meet a partner through a friend, match making, or activities that involve beauty or art.

Eighth-House Venus

Venus in the relocated eighth house can help you use money to make money, be successful with investments, or find gratification in sexual pursuits, emotional encounters, or looking beneath the surface of life. You could meet someone special through therapy, investment activities, research, or while studying metaphysics.

Ninth-House Venus

Travel, higher education, philosophy, religion, or activities that involve inspiration and looking for a higher truth are more gratifying when Venus is in the relocated ninth house. You might meet someone special in or from another country, in class, on the road, or when you're seeking answers about the ultimate meaning of life.

Tenth-House Venus

When Venus is in the relocated tenth house, you can improve relationships with authority figures, get along better with the boss, or gain more gratification from your career. You may become more diplomatic and could encounter a romantic partner through professional activities, a mentor, or while managing a major project.

Eleventh-House Venus

With Venus in the relocated eleventh house, you can widen your circle of acquaintances and find pleasure through groups, humanitarian activities, or community action. Satisfaction could come through new ideas or unusual perspectives, and you might meet a partner through a group, organization, friend, or chance encounter.

Twelfth-House Venus

If you want to explore the world of beauty, enjoy meditation or other spiritual pursuits, or bring comfort to the less fortunate, Venus in the relocated twelfth house is a plus. You might meet someone special in an institution (hospital, prison), a sheltered place (ashram, monastery, church, temple), or a naturally beautiful location, or through activities that accent grace and imagination.

Mars

First-House Mars

Mars in the relocated first house is an advantage if you want more physical energy, to compete in sports, or to develop more initiative, independence, or a pioneering spirit. However, if strife, conflict, or irritation already come easily to you, this is probably a placement to avoid.

Second-House Mars

With Mars in the relocated second house, you devote more energy to the pursuit of money, possessions, and other material goods. This placement also accents your sensuality, and can help you develop more endurance and cultivate more patience and perseverance.

Third-House Mars

With Mars in the relocated third house, you can sharpen your wits, develop a comedic bent, become more active in the neighborhood, declare your independence from siblings, or encourage physical dexterity and flexibility. Be cautious, though; in this location your words can become weapons—biting, ironic, sarcastic, and hurtful to others.

Fourth-House Mars

When Mars is in the relocated fourth house, you could be more active in the home environment, stir things up in your domestic realm, challenge family members, or take the initiative to nurture and protect loved ones. If family members easily spark irritability—or anger—however, you might want to bypass this location.

Fifth-House Mars

If you want to encourage your dramatic instincts, creativity, or ability to shine, Mars in the relocated fifth house can help you succeed. You might receive more personal recognition, or become more active with children, love affairs, the entertainment world, speculation, or activities involving excitement, risk, or potential financial gain.

Sixth-House Mars

When Mars is in the relocated sixth house, you want to be more personally and professionally productive and effective, and be of service to others. You may utilize more of your initiative and pioneering spirit on the job, but if you tend to be self-critical or work to excess, this is an inadvisable move.

Seventh-House Mars

Added sex appeal, action, and liveliness in your partnerships are possible with Mars in the relocated seventh house. But there's also more competition, or arguing, if issues of self-centeredness arise in relationships. The balancing act between assertion and cooperation is featured. If you tend to give your power to other people, this is an inadvisable placement.

Eighth-House Mars

Mars in the relocated eighth house can be beneficial if you want more emotional intensity or emphasis on sexuality or shared resources. In this location you can take the initiative to look beneath the surface of life, be courageous, or confront deep-seated or subconscious issues. Avoid this placement if you and your partner disagree about finances.

Ninth-House Mars

When Mars is in the relocated ninth house, you want more adventures and are interested in knowledge and in exploring and seeing the world. You also could be very active in education, religion, philosophy, other cultures, or those things that bring enlightenment and broaden your horizons. Self-confidence and extroversion could increase.

Tenth-House Mars

Mars in the relocated tenth house can help you take charge of your career, fulfill your entrepreneurial aspirations, and generate more action, leadership, or independence in your vocation. If you're inclined to butt heads with bosses, this is a placement to avoid. High energy, accomplishments, and increased status are accentuated.

Eleventh-House Mars

When Mars is in the relocated eleventh house, you're eager to become more active in groups, organizations, or humanitarian causes, or with friends. Your willingness to fight for progress could increase, and you may be avid in your exploration of fresh opportunities where you can be a leader. Independence is highlighted.

Twelfth-House Mars

Mars in the relocated twelfth house is a plus if you're interested in meditation, fighting for a spiritual cause, or putting lots of energy into compassionate or philanthropic activities. You may develop the ability to put grace into motion (dancing, skating, tai chi, etc.). Personal ideals are highlighted. You seek the best for yourself and others.

Jupiter

First-House Jupiter

If more optimism, self-confidence, or vitality is your quest, you could fulfill your desire with Jupiter in the relocated first house. You may become more interested in a religion, philosophy, belief system, or set of ideals, and expand yourself personally and physically (weight gain is possible). More faith and a willingness to risk for greater gain also are possible.

Second-House Jupiter

Jupiter in the relocated second house could help you succeed if you're looking for opportunities to expand your material base, money, and possessions. But this placement also encourages spending and extravagance. You're apt to place a higher priority on comfort, pleasure, and gratification from the physical world in this location.

Third-House Jupiter

With Jupiter in the relocated third house, you want more mental stimulation and can accentuate your abilities as a teacher, communicator, or writer. Your sense of humor could become quicker and more expressive, and your verbal skills are apt to increase. The urge to travel may also grow. Physical and mental restlessness are featured.

Fourth-House Jupiter

Jupiter in the relocated fourth house is a plus if your goal is a larger, renovated or retirement home or one filled with books, philosophical discussions, or interesting people from faraway places. High ideals could be tied to family members or your attitudes about nurturing, and good fortune and lucky contacts could come through family members.

Fifth-House Jupiter

When Jupiter is in the relocated fifth house, you may be more interested in children, entertainment, sports, hobbies, or taking center stage in a big way. Gambling and risk taking are accentuated, but success is not guaranteed, so temper your actions with caution. You could have more romantic opportunities in this location.

Sixth-House Jupiter

When Jupiter is in the relocated sixth house, you increase your productivity and efficiency. This placement also favors work involving ideals, philosophy, exploration, writing, adventure, and expanding your mental or physical horizons. Jupiter here may strengthen physical vitality and recuperative abilities as well as work volume.

Seventh-House Jupiter

Jupiter in the relocated seventh house is a plus for good times, fellowship, and confidence in partnerships. You seek the best in love relationships or are attracted to people who are optimistic, intelligent, humorous, interested in a higher truth, or strongly idealistic. You also might expect more than is reasonable from others.

Eighth-House Jupiter

With Jupiter in the relocated eighth house, you can expand your capacity for intimacy, sexuality, or joint resources. You may become excited about exploring psychotherapy, metaphysical subjects, or other hidden matters. Both depth and breadth prevail in research, and you could benefit from the generosity of others.

Ninth-House Jupiter

If you want more focus on enlightenment, philosophy, religion, travel, adventure, and exploration, Jupiter in the relocated ninth house can bring you closer to your goal. Growth, development, and expansion are accentuated, as are faith and optimism. Idealism may also rise, which can be positive or negative; give yourself a periodic reality check.

Tenth-House Jupiter

Jupiter in the relocated tenth house can bring professional luck and opportunities through fortunate connections. In this location, you could take the next step—or several steps—up in status. Education increases the chance for success, and your employer could foot the bill, considering it an investment in your and the company's future.

Eleventh-House Jupiter

Intellectual sharpness and progressive ideas are featured when Jupiter is in the relocated eleventh house, as is increasing your circle of friends and increased activity in an organization or a humanitarian cause. Your desire for independence is likely to increase, and networking brings you closer to your personal and professional goals.

Twelfth-House Jupiter

Jupiter in the relocated twelfth house can increase your unconscious faith, bringing a sense of having a guardian angel looking over you. You also could have more mystical experiences, an enlarged sense of compassion, or greater involvement in seeking a higher truth and ultimate meaning. Metaphysical studies can help you tune in to your sixth sense.

Saturn

First-House Saturn

Saturn in the relocated first house is an asset if you want to work harder, learn important personal life lessons, become more responsible or practical, or deal with issues related to authority and control. However, this placement is inadvisable if you have a tendency toward health problems or are somewhat self-critical.

Second-House Saturn

Moving Saturn into the relocated second house can help you become more practical and responsible in money matters, but if overdone, this placement can indicate self-denial, poverty consciousness, and lack of pleasure. The discipline indicated by Saturn must be handled with care when applied to sensuality and comfort, as it is here.

Third-House Saturn

Saturn in the relocated third house aids concentration and practicality and encourages tangible mental output, such as writing. But if you tend to have a strong inner critic in intellectual matters, this placement is apt to simply increase the tendency. You may take on more responsibility for siblings or other relatives.

Fourth-House Saturn

With Saturn in the relocated fourth house, you seek more reliability and stability on the home front, and a home-based business or working with family members is possible. However, if criticism involving loved ones is more the norm than the exception, this is a placement to avoid. Parenting skills are accentuated, and you may carry more of the load with relatives.

Fifth-House Saturn

Saturn in the relocated fifth house can help you branch out personally and professionally in areas that involve more recognition, leadership, interaction with children or loved ones, the entertainment world, long-term investments, or speculation. If you doubt your creativity, however, this is probably a location to avoid.

Sixth-House Saturn

With Saturn in the relocated sixth house, you want more tangible results in your daily work or are looking to be more practical, responsible, dedicated, and hardworking. On the down side, health problems can be associated with this placement, as can overwork, so an emphasis on a healthy, balanced lifestyle is to your advantage.

Seventh-House Saturn

If you want to be more sensible about relationships and put more effort into partnerships, Saturn in the relocated seventh house assists your quest. This is not an advisable placement, however, if you tend to feel blocked from love or less loved than you would like, or are subject to criticism and control from partners or close relatives.

Eighth-House Saturn

Saturn in the relocated eighth house can boost self-mastery and self-control, and be helpful if you want to stop drinking or smoking or put an end to other bad habits. On the down side, power struggles over joint resources are possible, as are sexual blockages. With this location, it is wise to avoid taking on significant debt on your own or with a partner.

Ninth-House Saturn

When Saturn is in the relocated ninth house, your career could involve more travel, education, inspiration, or involvement with high ideals or big dreams. You might adopt a more practical attitude about philosophies and religion, but an existential crisis is also a possibility.

Tenth-House Saturn

If you want more responsibility or power on the job, Saturn in the relocated tenth house can bring you closer to your goal. You may work more productively or within the establishment. If critical, harsh, or overly demanding bosses are the norm for you, this is a placement to avoid. Paternal motifs also are highlighted.

Eleventh-House Saturn

When Saturn is in the relocated eleventh house, you incorporate more common sense into friendships and associations. You may initiate change and take charge in groups or use technology and new concepts in practical ways. If your originality is usually stifled, this is a placement to avoid.

Twelfth-House Saturn

With Saturn in the relocated twelfth house, you seek more definition and clarity in the mystical realm, and may bring beauty, inspiration, imagination, or compassion to your profession. If you tend toward excessively high ideals or perfectionism, this placement is probably inadvisable.

Uranus

First-House Uranus

If you seek more independence, originality, or an inventive spirit, Uranus in the relocated first house can help you access that energy. This placement also encourages your unconventional side, but if you're accident-prone or a "rebel without a cause," this is a placement to avoid.

Second-House Uranus

Uranus in the relocated second house can assist you in earning money through astrology or new technology, or by working unusual hours or in a unique field or fashion. Self-employment is a possibility. But beware of this placement if you're uncomfortable with an erratic, unpredictable income.

Third-House Uranus

Uranus in the relocated third house is a great influence if you want to increase your ability to find unique solutions and be viewed as an idea person. This placement also encourages brainstorming and the ability to look at personal and professional events and situations with a fresh, innovative perspective. Flashes of insight are possible. Serendipitous moments may occur more often.

Fourth-House Uranus

Uranus in the relocated fourth house is almost guaranteed to stir things up on the home front. It could manifest in the form of ongoing change, unusual people, or odd and eccentric behaviors. If emotional, family, and physical security are very important to you, you probably would be uncomfortable with this placement.

Fifth-House Uranus

Uranus in the relocated fifth house signals more excitement and thrills in your personal and love lives. Creativity and originality are likely to be enhanced, and love affairs could start—and end—suddenly. The tendency to take risks is heightened, so try to be cautious with investments and speculation if you find yourself in this location.

Sixth-House Uranus

With Uranus in the relocated sixth house, you want more freedom in your day-to-day work and might be ready to accept a nonstandard shift or follow an unconventional routine on the job. You will gravitate toward more variety and a willingness to challenge the powers that be. This placement can bring sudden changes on the job.

Seventh-House Uranus

When Uranus is in the relocated seventh house, you want more variety, change, and excitement in your relationships and may attract people who are rather unusual. If you have problems with commitment or tend to attract people who feel trapped when in a relationship, this is a placement to avoid. Erratic partnerships and sudden breakups are possible.

Eighth-House Uranus

If your preference is a more open-ended approach to intimacy, or you want to spice up your sex life, Uranus in the relocated eighth house could fulfill your desire. You also could be motivated to try unconventional approaches in joint resources and sharing money and possessions, but stop short of putting your financial security at risk.

Ninth-House Uranus

If you want to be more adventurous or are eager to explore new horizons and unconventional concepts, Uranus in the relocated ninth house encourages your quest. You may question religious or educational authority figures in this location. This placement is also a positive influence for seeking unusual or technological knowledge.

Tenth-House Uranus

If you're ready to start a personal professional revolution, Uranus in the relocated tenth house provides the incentive. Here, you can make a break from an old career, venture into a new field, or use new technology or inventive skills within your vocation. If follow-through in professional commitments is an issue, this is not the placement for you.

Eleventh-House Uranus

Uranus in the relocated eleventh house can help you enlarge your circle of friends and acquaintances, increase opportunities to view things from different perspectives, strengthen humanitarian urges, and reinforce your interest in what is new and on the cutting edge of change. Personal freedom moves higher on the priority list.

Twelfth-House Uranus

If you are seeking something a bit different in terms of mystical experiences, compassionate activities, imaginative pursuits, or your relationship with nature, Uranus in the relocated twelfth house is a helpful placement. An avant-garde attitude about art and beauty is possible, and sudden psychic flashes of insight could occur.

Neptune

First-House Neptune

With Neptune in the relocated first house, you can increase personal grace, beauty, charisma, and artistic ability. Imagination and inspiration are accented. However, physical sensitivity could increase, especially to drugs, alcohol, and environmental influences. This placement also signals adaptability and the talent to "fit in" in almost any situation.

Second-House Neptune

Neptune in the relocated second house can fulfill your wish if you want to make more money through art, visualization, compassion, or other inspired pursuits. Financial hunches can be profitable here, but deception is also possible. If income or money management is an issue, this location is probably one to avoid.

Third-House Neptune

When Neptune is in the relocated third house, your imagination is an asset, especially in writing, speaking, and hands-on projects. This placement could help you achieve greater fluency in other languages or inspire a gift for singing, song writing, or poetry. Deception could affect your relationships with siblings, relatives, and neighbors.

Fourth-House Neptune

Neptune in the relocated fourth house can be a positive influence if you desire a home near water or one that functions as your personal sanctuary. Emotional sensitivity, faith, and inspiration could increase. But if a family member has a drug or alcohol problem or sees you as a rescuer, this is probably a placement to avoid.

Fifth-House Neptune

When Neptune is in the relocated fifth house, you can earn more recognition for your imagination or compassion, and share dreams with children and loved ones. Creativity is heightened, and an artistic hobby could become a source of income. If you're a parent, nurture your children's creativity and talk with them about drugs and alcohol.

Sixth-House Neptune

If you want to turn your job-related dreams into reality, Neptune in the relocated sixth house can further your goal. This placement favors artists, craftspeople, helpers, and healers. Here, you can be idealistic and practical, assist the less fortunate, and work to make the world a better or more beautiful place. Avoid this placement if you tend to have mysterious ailments, low energy, or chronic health problems.

Seventh-House Neptune

When Neptune is in the relocated seventh house, you want to create a relationship that flows with beauty and harmony. This can manifest as love and romance, along with shared ideals and a tendency to see the best in each other. On the down side, deception, lies, illusion, or addictions (drugs, alcohol, etc.) can be a problem in partnerships.

Eighth-House Neptune

Neptune in the relocated eighth house increases the potential for sacred sexuality—exchanges that are deeply sensual as well as spiritual. Empathy and compassion may rule where shared resources are concerned, but on a less positive level, using and abusing one another or lies and confusion are possible, especially with money and sex.

Ninth-House Neptune

When Neptune is in the relocated ninth house, you want mystical and inspirational experiences, especially through nature, philosophy, or uplifting ideas. You may put more value on travel, education, or truth seeking. Some tension is likely when honesty clashes with idealism and results in "little white lies." Be true to yourself and your beliefs.

Tenth-House Neptune

Neptune in the relocated tenth house can help you bring more beauty, compassion, or imagination into your professional life. Perhaps it's time to follow your dream and pursue a new career. However, try to avoid this placement if your norm is deceptive or confused bosses or jobs that dissolve and disappear.

Eleventh-House Neptune

With Neptune in the relocated eleventh house, you can develop friendships based on ideals and dreams, and humanitarian instincts may be heightened. Too much compassion, however, can lead to codependency. Art, beauty, or mystical matters may be the focus of discussion and activities with groups, organizations, and friends.

Twelfth-House Neptune

If you seek a deeper connection to universal truths, yearn for more mystical experiences, or want to increase your psychic ability, Neptune in the relocated twelfth house can open the pathway. Heightened compassion and sensitivity are possible. Or you might feel confused, lost in fantasy, or caught up in habit patterns or the lies of others.

Pluto

First-House Pluto

With Pluto in the relocated first house, you can increase your physical stamina or develop more self-discipline and inner mastery. In this location it's easier to transform yourself, to turn negative habits into positive ones. However, expect power issues to emerge, both in yourself and others.

Second-House Pluto

If you want to use money to make money, establish a consulting or freelance income, or earn money through therapy, life-and-death issues, or any vocation that focuses on intense emotions or delves beneath the surface of life, Pluto in the relocated second house can be helpful. Major earnings are possible, but so is financial loss.

Third-House Pluto

When Pluto is in the relocated third house, you want more intensity and focus in your intellectual life. Research skills, concentration, and analytical ability are strengthened, and mental tenacity helps you see projects through to completion. Be cautious, though, of tunnel vision and obsessive thinking.

Fourth-House Pluto

With Pluto in the relocated fourth house, major renovations or transformations within the domestic arena are likely. Possibilities include refurbishing old homes, or emotional upheavals and radical shifts within the family. In this location you also could work through childhood issues or research your roots.

Fifth-House Pluto

A stronger sexual focus and an intense approach to love and romance are likely when Pluto is in the relocated fifth house. In this location you also could delve deeply into the entertainment world (amateur or professional), recreation, or creative self-expression, which could help you access subconscious desires and needs.

Sixth-House Pluto

When Pluto is in the relocated sixth house, you desire more focus, concentration, and perseverance in your work life. Here, determination and the ability to complete major projects are enhanced. Keep a close eye on your work habits, however. In this location it's easy to push yourself too hard and to become obsessive.

Seventh-House Pluto

Pluto in the relocated seventh house accents strong reactions and interactions within partnerships, and highlights loyalty and commitment. Sensual and sexual gratification may become more important, but manipulation and power struggles concerning sex and money are highly possible.

Eighth-House Pluto

When Pluto is in the relocated eighth house, intense emotions may dominate nearly every facet of your life. Extremes and a "do or die" attitude are probable, and "feast or famine" experiences concerning food, sexuality, money, and resources are possible. Willpower and strength of purpose are accentuated.

Ninth-House Pluto

Pluto in the relocated ninth house is likely to trigger intense emotions concerning philosophy, religion, the meaning of life, or truth seeking. In this location you question beliefs and values, and dig deeply to find the life philosophy that works for you. This location also can be positive for research projects and higher education because it aids concentration.

Tenth-House Pluto

With Pluto in the relocated tenth house, you seek mastery and control within your career and may eliminate certain aspects of your professional life. A vocation involving therapy, joint resources, money, metaphysics, or areas that arouse intense emotion is possible. If you have power issues with bosses, this placement is inadvisable.

Eleventh-House Pluto

If you seek a stronger, deeper commitment to friends, humanitarian causes, or the wider world, Pluto in the relocated eleventh house can help you achieve your aim. You could turn friends into mates and partners (and vice versa). But expect some tension when freedom urges and intimacy instincts clash.

Twelfth-House Pluto

When Pluto is in the relocated twelfth house, you seek more privacy and time alone, and the urge to explore your subconscious is likely. In this location the tendency is to delve more and more deeply into yourself and mystical, transcendent realms. Cathartic artistic and personal experiences are possible.

8
Ruling Planets
Aspecting Angles

Planets actually do "double duty" in a chart. Each planet symbolizes basic universal drives and life activities (see chapters 1 and 2) and also operates as a sort of "representative" for one or more of the twelve houses in every chart. Astrologers use these planetary rulerships to interpret the empty houses (those that contain no planets) in a chart, as well as those in which planets are found.

To review this concept, which was explained in chapter 1: Each sign is associated with a planet, called its ruler. Because there is a sign on the cusp (dividing line between two houses) of each house, the planet associated with that sign therefore rules that house, serving as the representative for matters governed by that house. This principle also applies to houses that contain planets, so every house has a ruling planet, whether it is empty or contains several planets.

As an example, suppose relationships have been a bit of a dry spot in your life. One option is to move to an area where Venus is in your relocated seventh house (relationships, marriage, and partnership). But suppose that location is one you have no desire to visit, much less live in. Planetary rulerships can provide the solution.

To boost your chances for a relationship, you could move to a location where the planet ruling the relocated seventh house is in harmonious aspect to one of the angles

(Ascendant, Descendant, Midheaven, IC). For example, if your relocated Descendant is in Leo, ruled by the Sun, you would want the Sun to be in a sextile or trine aspect to one of the angles.

Finding such a location is not as improbable as it might seem at first glance. Remember, each sign has 30°, which represents about 3,000 miles, or the approximate coast-to-coast distance of the continental United States. This gives you lots of options. Remember also that the Ascendant/Descendant axis does not move, and thus change signs, as quickly. But you might be lucky and find a location where Venus is trine or sextile the Descendant—even better!

If it's still difficult to find a location in which you want to live where the Sun, in this example, aspects an angle, there is yet another alternative. Find the planet in your birth chart (birth location) that has the most harmonious aspects. Then put the sign ruled by that planet on the relocated Descendant, or that planet in the relocated seventh house.

Yet another alternative is to use a house's co-ruler. The planet ruling the sign that begins somewhere within a house, and is usually on the cusp of the succeeding house, is called that house's co-ruler. For example, if Leo is on the cusp of the seventh house, Virgo begins in the seventh house and is on the cusp of the eighth house. (The exception involves what is called an intercepted sign, or a sign wholly contained within a single house. When this occurs, two houses have the same sign on the cusp.)

You can emphasize any area of life in this way, or by having multiple planets in the appropriate house.

Signs and Ruling Planets

Signs	*Ruling Planet(s)*
Aries ♈	Mars ♂
Taurus ♉	Venus ♀
Gemini ♊	Mercury ☿
Cancer ♋	Moon ☽
Leo ♌	Sun ☉
Virgo ♍	Mercury ☿
Libra ♎	Venus ♀
Scorpio ♏	Mars ♂, Pluto ♇
Sagittarius ♐	Jupiter ♃
Capricorn ♑	Saturn ♄
Aquarius ♒	Saturn ♄, Uranus ♅
Pisces ♓	Jupiter ♃, Neptune ♆

To illustrate, here are a few examples:

One woman was born with a Capricorn Ascendant, and Ascendant-ruler Saturn in a water sign. She moved to a location where Sagittarius is the relocated Ascendant; Jupiter, which rules Sagittarius, is conjunct the Sun and Mercury. As a result, she is much more articulate, witty, entertaining, and outgoing in that locale.

Another woman's birth chart has a Sagittarius Ascendant; Jupiter, the ruler, is in Aries in the third house. (She has been a voracious reader all her life.) Scorpio is the Ascendant in her relocated chart; Pluto, the ruler, is in the eighth house. She moved to a location to be with her brother, a psychotherapist, and has had a number of eighth-house experiences, such as life-and-death issues and increased activity concerning shared resources.

A man excelled in his professional life in a location that put the ruler of his Midheaven in the second house and trine the Midheaven. The Midheaven ruler is also his Ascendant ruler in that location.

A woman moved from a location with a Taurus Ascendant to one with an Aries Ascendant. Mars, the ruler of the Aries Ascendant, is in the fifth house in that location, and she has four children.

Now identify the ruling planets of each of the houses in your birth chart and those that harmoniously (sextile, trine) aspect the angles. Then do the same for your relocated chart(s) and read the descriptions that follow.

Rulers in Harmonious Aspect to the Angles

First-House Ruler Sextile/Trine Ascendant/Descendant

With the ruler of your first house in harmony with the Ascendant/Descendant, you could have more energy and vitality, improved health or a healthier lifestyle, the incentive to go after what you want in life, added initiative and confidence, and the motivation to comfortably share your world with a partner. The balance between self and other may flow more smoothly, with an emphasis on compromise.

First-House Ruler Sextile/Trine Midheaven/IC

With the ruler of your first house in harmony with the Midheaven/IC, you could invest more of your energy in your career or tune in to your entrepreneurial side. You also could better meet your and your family's needs, achieve your aims despite personal and professional limitations, and develop better relationships with parents or other authority figures. Here, you may find it easier to balance independence and dependence, nurturing and career.

Second-House Ruler Sextile/Trine Ascendant/Descendant

When the ruler of your second house is in harmony with the Ascendant/Descendant, you could achieve more financial independence. You may become more sensual, instinctively seeking pleasure from the material world, and take the initiative to seek material goods. Pampering comes more easily in relationships, and financial teamwork is possible. A partner could increase your net worth, or you could provide important material support for a spouse. Agreement comes more easily concerning comfort, possessions, and pleasures.

Second-House Ruler Sextile/Trine Midheaven/IC

With the ruler of your second house in harmony with the Midheaven/IC, you may earn a higher income or work in a field with more income potential. You could gain more pleasure from your work, or achieve a better balance between ease and effort in your life. Here, your social status is favorable, financial matters might flow more smoothly with loved ones, and other people in your home may encourage you to please yourself. You could get some assistance (money or possessions) from parents or other family members.

Third-House Ruler Sextile/Trine Ascendant/Descendant

When the ruler of your third house is in harmony with the Ascendant/Descendant, your thinking may accelerate, and you have the opportunity to master the art of the quick quip and rapid repartee. You're likely to do more thinking, talking, learning, and sharing of information. Relatives could encourage you to be yourself, and communication is on the upswing in relationships, with an easy exchange of ideas. Objectivity and the ability to be lighthearted are assets within partnerships.

Third-House Ruler Sextile/Trine Midheaven/IC

When the ruler of your third house is in harmony with the Midheaven/IC, you can use your mental skills to advance your career. You may think, talk, or learn more within your profession, and a relative might assist to you in terms of work or status. Flexibility, dexterity, and multitasking are likely assets in your vocational life, and you may find it easier to communicate with authority figures and family members. Lively discussions are likely, and you could achieve a better balance between listening and talking. A parent may encourage you to learn more, both informally and to advance your career.

Fourth-House Ruler Sextile/Trine Ascendant/Descendant

With the ruler of your fourth house in harmony with the Ascendant/Descendant, you're likely to find a happy balance between caring for yourself and others. A mutual support system with family members is probable, and you can protect and be protected. Here, you can be yourself and pursue your own interests, and still spend quality time with family. Mutual nurturing is possible in relationships, where sharing and caring are accentuated. When appropriate and healthy, you can allow yourself to be vulnerable and assisted by others. You may find it easier to combine the roles of parent and partner.

Fourth-House Ruler Sextile/Trine Midheaven/IC

When the ruler of your fourth house is in harmony with the Midheaven/IC, you may achieve a better balance between your public and private lives, successfully managing a career and a domestic/family life. Supportive, caretaking motifs are accentuated for both you and loved ones, and the need to seek security is strengthened. Family members may be of assistance to you professionally, and you could establish a home-based business or pursue vocational interests in partnership with family members.

Fifth-House Ruler Sextile/Trine Ascendant/Descendant

When the ruler of your fifth house is in harmony with the Ascendant/Descendant, you may be more vivacious and outgoing. Your natural charisma is accentuated, and you could become more creative or discover a talent for amusing and entertaining others. Your energy flows naturally toward exciting pursuits, and relationships with loved ones and children may become more harmonious. Here, you can increase your self-esteem and may find it easier to shine and be noticed. Giving and receiving love are emphasized. You can successfully balance your roles as an equal and The Star.

Fifth-House Ruler Sextile/Trine Midheaven/IC

With the ruler of your fifth house in harmony with the Midheaven/IC, your confidence and charisma are likely to be vocational assets, and you can take risks for greater professional gains. You may earn more recognition or applause through your career, and children or loved ones could assist you or make a contribution to your work. Authority figures are likely to be impressed by your enthusiastic, dynamic approach, and family members find you more active, exciting, and fun.

Sixth-House Ruler Sextile/Trine Ascendant/Descendant

When the ruler of your sixth house is in harmony with the Ascendant/Descendant, much of your energy is devoted to working efficiently and effectively, and co-worker relationships could improve. You also might enhance your health or adopt a healthier lifestyle. Practical accomplishments could become more important to you, and skills for handling details, bringing order out of chaos, and fixing things could increase. Here, you can balance love and work, your partner may assist you in your work, or your job could contribute to or enhance your relationships. You may be more practical or successful in relating to people.

Sixth-House Ruler Sextile/Trine Midheaven/IC

When the ruler of your sixth house is in harmony with the Midheaven/IC, you may be more competent, efficient, or productive. In this location you find it easier to focus on facts, handle details, and be efficient on the job. The desire for tangible accomplishments is highlighted, and you excel at getting things done, both at home and on the job. Your family may contribute to your work success, and you can provide both emotional and practical support to loved ones. Here, you can achieve a good balance between work and family and domestic activities.

Seventh-House Ruler Sextile/Trine Ascendant/Descendant

When the ruler of your seventh house is in harmony with the Ascendant/Descendant, relationships may flow more smoothly. You may find it easier to meet people, including potential partners, in this location, where you can achieve a better balance between personal and interpersonal needs, between fulfilling your desires and pleasing other people. Cooperation and teamwork are easier. You may become more physically graceful or be more active in artistic or aesthetic pursuits. Negotiating and diplomatic skills could increase.

Seventh-House Ruler Sextile/Trine Midheaven/IC

With the ruler of your seventh house in harmony with the Midheaven/IC, you can achieve a better balance between relationships and career ambitions, and find a happy medium between being a peer and taking charge and running the show. Partners may contribute to your professional success. Your interpersonal skills could be an asset vocationally. Relationships with authority figures (including parents) and family members could improve, and you can move appropriately between the roles of partner and equal, dependent, nurturer, and executive or leader. Connections between a partner and family members may be enhanced.

Eighth-House Ruler Sextile/Trine Ascendant/Descendant

With the ruler of your eighth house in harmony with the Ascendant/Descendant, your emotions may feel more intense. Energy flows easily into intimacy or the pursuit of joint resources, and passions could rise. You and your partner may achieve more agreement and compromise regarding shared finances and possessions. Here, your ability to look beneath the surface helps you understand yourself and others more completely, and the relationship focus could become deeper and more committed. Loyalty is highlighted. The drive for sharing is accentuated.

Eighth-House Ruler Sextile/Trine Midheaven/IC

When the ruler of your eighth house is in harmony with the Midheaven/IC, your awareness of what is hidden (nonverbal cues, innuendoes, scandals) might become a professional asset, as could your research ability or aptitude for handling joint resources. Agreement with authority figures about "perks" and salary could come more easily. Intensified commitment to career achievement and caring connections within the home is possible, and a mate could provide vocational assistance. Perseverance contributes to your success, and intuition is helpful at home and on the job.

Ninth-House Ruler Sextile/Trine Ascendant/Descendant

With the ruler of your ninth house in harmony with the Ascendant/Descendant, you could become more confident and outgoing, and may feel the urge to travel more, take classes, or explore philosophy, religion, or other paths to ultimate truth. You may receive personal assistance from in-laws, spiritual leaders, or people from other countries or cultures. Here, you can be more optimistic and seek opportunities. You and a partner may find more common ground regarding beliefs and values, and shared ideals are likely as the two of you are apt to encourage the best in each other. The quest for excitement and adventure in relationships is highlighted.

Ninth-House Ruler Sextile/Trine Midheaven/IC

When the ruler of your ninth house is in harmony with the Midheaven/IC, your confidence and ability to visualize big dreams and schemes could prove to be vocational assets. Your faith and willingness to risk for greater gain may help you advance professionally, as could additional education or training or support from in-laws. In this location you're more willing to explore and venture into new territory in reaching for success and in nourishing and nurturing a family. You may decide to enlarge your home, travel more, or fill your home with exciting people or fresh, new ideas.

Tenth-House Ruler Sextile/Trine Ascendant/Descendant

When the ruler of your tenth house is in harmony with the Ascendant/Descendant, you devote much energy to career achievement and rising to the top. You're likely to be more practical, responsible, dedicated, and oriented toward tangible results. Relationships with authority figures may improve, and you might find it easier to pursue your personal desires within the realistic limits of the world while balancing your love and work lives. Your career and relationships may support one another, and you're effective as a co-worker and as an executive or leader. You can keep people happy while getting the job done well.

Tenth-House Ruler Sextile/Trine Midheaven/IC

When the ruler of your tenth house is in harmony with the Midheaven/IC, success may come more easily. Your executive instincts are highlighted, you can be more responsible, pragmatic, and achievement-oriented, and you may work a bit more or harder in this location. Here, you gravitate toward more control and power in your career, and may improve your relationships with authority figures. A good balance is possible between domestic duties and the demands of the outer world; you can combine competence and compassion. Your family may be more supportive of your ambitions, and you're likely to seek more security both at work and at home.

Eleventh-House Ruler Sextile/Trine Ascendant/Descendant

When the ruler of your eleventh house is in harmony with the Ascendant/Descendant, you may want more freedom or opportunities to exercise your inventiveness and express your individuality. Friends could become more important in your life, and you could become more active in groups and organizations. Your interest in technology could increase. Here, you're more willing to break the rules, to be a rebel, and your energy flows toward what is unusual and different; you also can encourage others to express their unique qualities. Friends and partners may assist each other (or people may move more easily between those roles), cooperation is accentuated, and objectivity is an asset in relationships, where you're mastering the art of love with freedom.

Eleventh-House Ruler Sextile/Trine Midheaven/IC

With the ruler of your eleventh house in harmony with the Midheaven/IC, your inventive genius can contribute to your success in the outer world. Technological skills, groups, organizations, networking, or anything on the cutting edge of change could help you advance professionally. Friends may prove helpful to your career. You can find a good balance between the conventional and unconventional, knowing when to work within the system and when to break the rules. Family members may encourage your individuality as you encourage theirs, and an open-minded attitude and mutual tolerance help domestic relationships flow more smoothly.

Twelfth-House Ruler Sextile/Trine Ascendant/Descendant

When the ruler of your twelfth house is in harmony with the Ascendant/Descendant, your personal drive flows easily into artistic, healing, charitable, or spiritual activities. Idealism is on the rise, and you want to do something to make the world a better or more beautiful place. You could enhance your physical attractiveness or become more graceful, and your imagination is in full flower. You may find yourself acting directly on intuition without knowing why. Shared dreams strengthen partnerships, and you and your mate naturally visualize—and feed—the highest potentials in one another.

Twelfth-House Ruler Sextile/Trine Midheaven/IC

When the ruler of your twelfth house is in harmony with the Midheaven/IC, your ability to visualize can be a professional asset. You may use your intuition, compassion, artistic talent, or healing ability more in your career, and can visualize a goal and work hard to bring it into form. Here, you have high standards for yourself as a worker, and want to contribute to society. The urge to beautify your domestic environment is possible, and you can turn your home into a sanctuary, a place that feeds your soul. Your sensitive side is extra supportive of loved ones, and you may encourage family members to explore mystical areas, philanthropic pursuits, or areas that uplift and inspire them.

9
Romance

Love and romance often appear at the least expected moment and in the least likely location. Sometimes a move is all it takes to shift the planetary energy into more positive territory. These are the influences to look for in relocating a birth chart to help attract romance, love, and marriage:

Romance

- Sun or Venus conjunct, sextile, or trine an angle
- Fifth-house ruler or co-ruler conjunct, sextile, or trine an angle
- Several planets in the fifth house

Love

- Venus, Sun, or Moon conjunct, trine, or sextile an angle, especially the Ascendant, Descendant, or IC
- Harmonious aspects between the rulers or co-rulers of the fifth, seventh, and eighth houses
- Harmonious aspects between the rulers or co-rulers of the fifth, seventh, and eighth houses and the Sun, Moon, or Venus

Marriage

- Venus conjunct, sextile, or trine an angle
- Seventh-house ruler or co-ruler conjunct, sextile, or trine an angle
- Seventh-house ruler or co-ruler sextile or trine Venus or planet(s) in the seventh house
- Several planets in the seventh house

It's unlikely to find all of these conditions active in one chart in one place. So, the more influences, the better the chances for finding love, romance, and/or marriage.

Lynn

Lynn moved from her birthplace to Seattle after graduating with a nursing degree. There, she launched her career with an excellent job at a hospital, and began to establish roots. From the outset, however, she found it difficult to meet people outside the work-place and had little luck in affairs of the heart. Her one long-term romance, which appeared to be headed toward marriage, ended after her partner got cold feet.

With Uranus-ruled Aquarius on the Descendant and Mercury in the seventh house in her birth chart (chart 9), Lynn values communication and independence in a relationship and wants a partner who also is her best friend. The Venus squares to Uranus and Pluto show the need for excitement and an attraction to unusual people, as well as the potential for sudden beginnings and endings, and transformative relationships. With Venus in the fifth house, romance is an important component of any relationship. Yet, Venus in the fifth square the Descendant ruler reflects the difficulty in taking a dating relationship to the next level—marriage.

Mercury square Neptune encourages Lynn to see relationships as she wishes them to be, not necessarily as they are, and reinforces her need for romance. This aspect also can indicate deception, and she felt very much deceived when the long-term relationship ended.

Besides having the Sun, Mercury, and the Descendant in freedom-loving Aquarius, Lynn has the Moon and Venus in Sagittarius, another sign that values independence. It wasn't long before she began to realize that many men were threatened by her self-suffi-ciency. Unwilling to compromise her values, she moved on and continued looking. This was particularly difficult for Lynn because her Ascendant-ruler, the Sun, is conjunct the

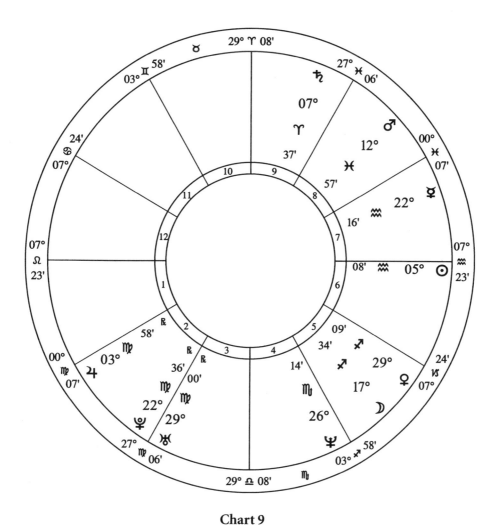

Chart 9
Lynn, Birth Chart
January 25, 1968 / Phoenix, AZ / 5:59 PM MST +7:00
Placidus Houses

Descendant, reflecting a strong need for someone with whom to share her life. The Moon is square Mars, Pluto, and Uranus, indicating emotional intensity.

Lynn's chart relocated to Seattle is nearly the same as her birth chart. The few changes only compounded the birth chart indicators. Pluto changed houses to the third and became the ruling planet of the fifth, where the sign on the cusp changed to Scorpio. That resulted in squares involving the fifth house of romance (Venus), the birth chart Descendant ruler (Uranus), and the relocated fifth-house ruler (Pluto). This effectively "erased" the advantage of the birth chart fifth-house ruler, Jupiter, in a trine with Venus (out-of-sign, and thus weak, with Venus in the final degree of Sagittarius and Jupiter in an early degree of Virgo). Friendships were few because Venus rules the relocated eleventh house (friends), with Taurus on the cusp.

A few years after the long-term relationship ended, Lynn's career reached a turning point. She had moved into an administrative position because of a back injury, and, with no love life in sight and an increasing desire to marry and start a family, she decided to return to school for a master's degree at Georgetown University in Washington, D.C.

It wasn't long before Lynn's life did a turnabout, as the relocated chart (chart 10) shows. Friends and socializing filled the hours when she wasn't at school or studying. These are the changes in the relocated chart:

- Leo Ascendant changes to Virgo; Aquarius Descendant changes to Pisces
- Aries Midheaven changes to Gemini; Libra IC changes to Sagittarius
- Jupiter moves from the second house to the twelfth
- All planets change houses

The most prominent indicator of love and romance is the Sun in the relocated fifth house sextile the relocated fifth-house ruler Saturn, and trine/sextile the Midheaven/IC axis. Saturn also is sextile/trine the Midheaven/IC axis. The relocated chart also suggests marriage. The seventh-house co-ruler, Jupiter, is conjunct the Ascendant and trine Venus in the fourth house, and Mars is in the seventh house. Pisces on the Descendant also highlights romance.

The natal Venus-Uranus-Pluto squares are still present, but have shifted to a first/fourth-house (self and home and family) influence and, through house rulership, to the second (money), third (communication), sixth (work and health), and ninth (ed-

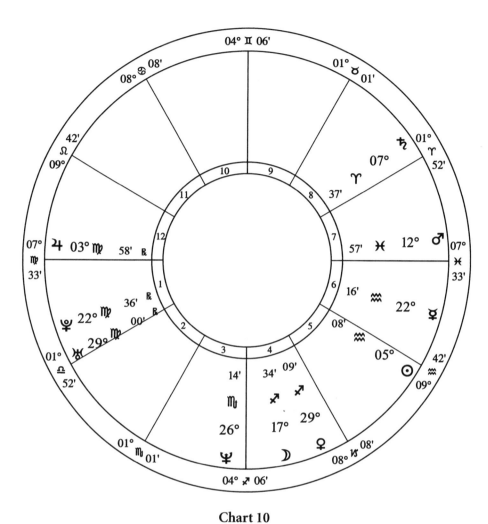

Chart 10
Lynn, Chart Relocated to Washington, D.C.
January 25, 1968 / Washington, D.C. / 5:59 PM MST +7:00
Placidus Houses

ucation, life philosophy) houses. With the added emphasis of the relocated fourth-house Moon square Mars, which is as passionate as it is potentially combative, it's important to stress compromise, joint decision-making, open communication, and time management to balance work and family life.

The outcome was that Lynn met her future husband through a mutual friend, and the couple married and decided to stay in the Washington, D.C., area, where they purchased a home and hope to start a family, as the Moon and Venus in the relocated fourth house indicate. Soon after moving in, Lynn and her husband found a positive outlet for the Moon- and Venus-Mars-Pluto-Uranus squares; they began home renovations and thus directed the energy into changing, transforming, and beautifying their surroundings.

Elizabeth Taylor

Elizabeth Taylor took her first step toward superstardom at age ten, when a movie scout spotted her at her father's art gallery in the Beverly Hills Hotel. This famous actress, who won her first Academy Award for *Butterfield 8,* is equally well-known for her often tumultuous love life.

Married eight times, including twice to fellow actor Richard Burton, Elizabeth's birth chart (chart 11) indicates multiple love affairs, weddings, and plenty of romance, all of which are even more easy to come by in the world of the silver screen. But this doesn't mean she was fated to have many short-lived marriages. It was her choice to respond that way to the planetary influences.

Love planet Venus, ruler of the fifth house of romance in Elizabeth's birth chart, is conjunct Uranus (change), and both are trine Jupiter (Ascendant ruler) and square Pluto. This is a good example of Jupiter's expansiveness; its influence exaggerated the number of multiple marriages already indicated by the Venus-Uranus conjunction in spontaneous Aries. Pluto contributes volatility, and its square to Venus can be an indication of relationships with unavailable people, such as Richard Burton, who was married to someone else when he and Elizabeth met. The Scorpio Moon-Pluto trine reflects deep emotions and a highly sexual nature.

The Gemini Descendant is ruled by Mercury, a sign and a planet that like variety and change almost as much as the Venus-Uranus conjunction. Mercury is conjunct action-oriented Mars and the Sun (self, ego), all in romantic Pisces. Neptune opposite the Pisces stellium takes Elizabeth's need for and love of romance to another level, while also

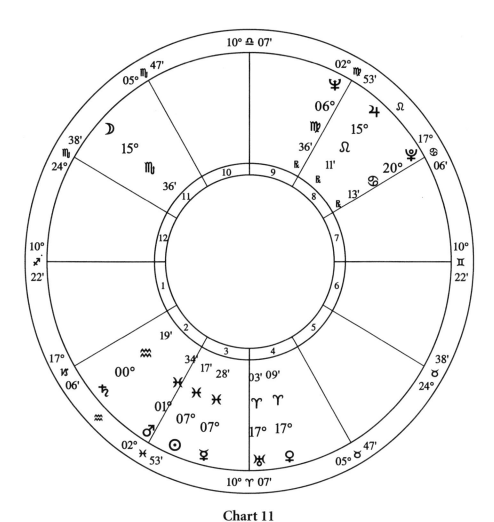

Chart 11
Elizabeth Taylor, Birth Chart
February 27, 1932 / London, England / 2:15 AM UT +0:00
Placidus Houses

leaving her open to deception and self-deceit—being in love with love. Once the romance associated with first love is gone, so is she, off to pursue new adventures spurred by the Sagittarius Ascendant trine its ruler, Jupiter, and Venus-Uranus.

As difficult a picture as Elizabeth's birth chart presents for relationships, it is all these factors that add up to her beauty, sex appeal, and charisma, and the indefinable qualities that make one person a Hollywood star and another a bit player.

Elizabeth Taylor and Richard Burton married the first time in Montreal, Canada, a location that emphasizes rather than minimizes the difficult relationship influences in her birth chart. These are the changes in the relocated chart (chart 12):

- Sagittarius Ascendant changes to Libra; Gemini Descendant changes to Aries
- Libra Midheaven changes to Cancer; Aries IC changes to Capricorn
- All house cusp signs change
- Mars, Sun, and Mercury are in the fifth house
- Venus and Uranus are conjunct the Descendant
- All other planets also change houses

Love, romance, and marriage are strongly accented in this location with three planets in the fifth house, including the Sun conjunct the relocated seventh-house ruler, Mars. Venus conjunct the Descendant is a wonderful aspect for relationships, but its conjunction to Uranus, ruler of the relocated fifth house, signals disruption as much as excitement, and it's placed in impatient, daring Aries.

Pluto, a planet that can signal abusive relationships, is conjunct the Midheaven, a placement that emphasizes power issues. With its square to the Venus-Uranus conjunction and the relocated Ascendant/Descendant axis, it's no surprise that Liz and Richard's fights reached epic proportions. This is reinforced by Aries, sign of the warrior, on the relocated Descendant, and the emotional intensity of the Scorpio Moon in the relocated first house trine Pluto and square Jupiter, which also is trine Venus-Uranus.

Is there a location where Elizabeth Taylor could begin a relationship or marry to increase her odds for success? Probably not. Notice how the Moon, Pluto, Jupiter, Venus, and Uranus are linked in a five-planet configuration tied to love and marriage. Wherever she is, the odds are that more than one of these planets will aspect the angles; if one is in harmonious aspect, another will be in hard aspect. Love affairs are her strength; marriage is not.

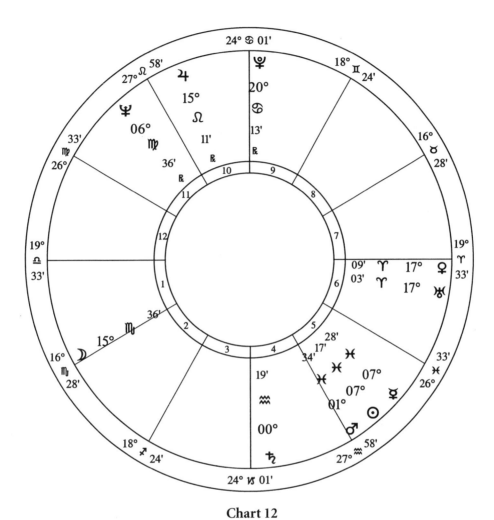

Chart 12
Elizabeth Taylor, Chart Relocated to Montreal, Canada
February 27, 1932 / Montreal, Canada / 2:15 AM UT +0:00
Placidus Houses

10
Career

The right company, the right connections, the right education and training, and the right location can define the difference between an average career and an outstanding one. You also can increase the odds for a rise in popularity or status—or even fame—by moving to an area where your relocated chart highlights one or more of the following influences.

Career Development

- Saturn sextile or trine the Midheaven
- Jupiter conjunct, sextile, or trine the Midheaven
- Pluto sextile or trine the Midheaven
- Sun conjunct, sextile, or trine the Midheaven
- The Midheaven ruler or co-ruler sextile or trine the Midheaven
- Planets in the tenth house

Status

- Saturn and/or Jupiter in the tenth house
- Saturn sextile or trine an angle

- Jupiter conjunct the Midheaven
- Jupiter sextile or trine an angle
- Sun conjunct, sextile, or trine the Midheaven

Bill Clinton

Former President Bill Clinton was born with all the planets in all the right places for a politician—or nearly so, because no chart and no person are perfect.

Born with the Sun in outgoing, exuberant, and determined Leo in the eleventh house of goals, friends, and groups, he's a natural leader who aims high and pushes himself to succeed (chart 13). The Sun sextile Jupiter reinforces the Leo confidence, and because Jupiter rules the third house of communication, he easily conveys his plans, ideas, and optimism to individuals, small groups, and audiences numbering in the thousands and millions.

Although it's difficult to pinpoint one skill that stands above the rest, one of Clinton's greatest strengths is undoubtedly one-on-one communication. His Ascendant is in Libra, the sign of relationships, and it benefits from all the charm and charisma of a Mars-Neptune-Venus stellium in Libra in the first house and conjunct the Ascendant. This is a powerful combination that reflects his ability to make anyone feel like the center of attention, even in casual conversation.

The Mars-Neptune-Venus stellium is square the Midheaven, so Clinton uses all his charm and charisma to further his career and to communicate with the public. But these squares also signal conflict (Mars), disillusionment and deceit (Neptune), and trouble through women (Venus).

The Libra Ascendant and stellium identify him as a passionate romantic who thrives on the chase and is prone to many love affairs. There is no question he attracts people, especially women, like a magnet, and he can charm most anyone into fulfilling his wishes. As an example, Pamela Harriman, widow of Averell Harriman, a former New York governor and U.S. ambassador, raised $12 million for Clinton's first presidential campaign.

The Mercury-Saturn-Pluto stellium is an aspect of intelligence, planning, intense thought, brooding, and analysis. Placed in the tenth and eleventh houses, Clinton is motivated and ambitious, and Saturn reflects his long-term plan to rise through the ranks and eventually become president of the United States, the most powerful (Pluto) position

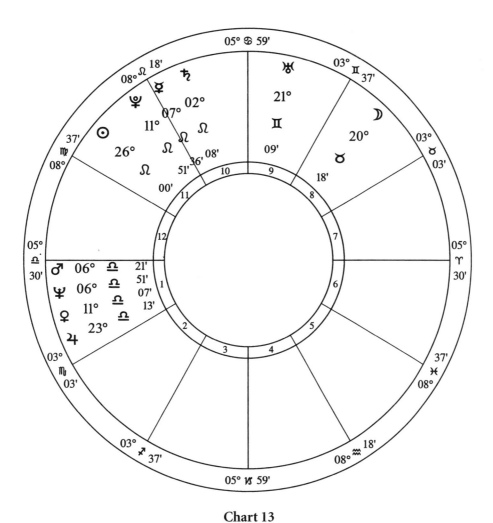

Chart 13
Bill Clinton, Birth Chart
August 19, 1946 / Hope, AR / 8:51 AM CST +6:00
Placidus Houses

on the planet. This desire germinated when, as a high school senior, he visited Washington, D.C., and met President John F. Kennedy.

But the Mercury-Saturn-Pluto stellium is in ego-driven Leo, so he can become too close to his ideas, develop tunnel vision, and never consider alternatives, because he believes he has the right—and only—solution. Because Saturn is often called the planet of karma, in addition to being known for its tough lessons, the negative tendencies represented by the stellium are ones Clinton has had to learn the hard way. To compound this, many of the lessons learned have occurred "in public" because of the tenth-house placement.

Besides the highly publicized Monica Lewinsky affair, Clinton lost his first reelection bid for Arkansas governor because he approved a vehicle license plate tax increase to fund education. Nevertheless, he made a comeback in the next election and again became governor.

Clinton biographer David Maraniss, author of *First in His Class*, says, "He has endured so many personal and political crises in his life and recovered from every one of them. It's just a habitual recovery process for him now. He starts out being angry, confused and depressed, and then slowly tries to find his way."[1]

From an astrological perspective, Maraniss' words accurately reflect Clinton's birth chart: Mars (anger) conjunct Neptune (confusion) sextile Mercury-Saturn-Pluto (depression, analysis, slow restart, transformation, and eventual success). Journalist Richard Lacayo writes, "Clinton has been famously open to compromise and tactical retreat,"[2] which aptly describes Clinton's Ascendant and Mars in Libra, as well as Venus and Neptune.

Clinton's lucky first-house Jupiter is even more so because of its sextile to the Sun and trine to Uranus. He connects with the people (Sun in the eleventh house) who can help him reach his goals and, often in unusual ways, being in the right place at the right time, as indicated by the Jupiter-Uranus trine, which is often a very fortunate aspect in astrology. Uranus also is sextile the Sun (self), setting up a three-planet link that places Clinton at the center, the recipient of all this bounty. With Uranus in the ninth house of legal matters and ruling the fifth house of love affairs, he was able to survive the impeachment trial that resulted from the Monica Lewinsky scandal.

The only square aspect in Clinton's chart is the Sun-Moon square. This aspect represents his father/stepfather (Sun) and mother (Moon), and the conflict that was present (his parents were divorced). Clinton's birth father died three months before Clinton was born, and his stepfather was an alcoholic who abused Clinton's mother. This is particularly evident in Clinton's chart because the Moon rules the tenth house, and Saturn rules the fourth, the two houses that represent parents. (Not everyone who has a Sun-Moon square will experience what Bill Clinton did in childhood.)

Unlike many presidents, Clinton was not a wealthy man when he entered the White House. Yet the Moon in materialistic, sensuous, comfort-loving Taurus in the eighth house of joint resources shows financial potential. And even though the Moon's square to the Sun somewhat blocks financial gain, it also motivates him to take action. This square is softened considerably by the Sun's harmonious aspects to Jupiter and Uranus, and Clinton used it to his advantage in seeking the support of friends and groups to help fund his campaigns.

There are few changes in Clinton's chart when relocated to Washington, D.C. (chart 14). Each is significant to his overwhelming popularity as well as to his near-downfall. The sign on each house cusp is the same, as are the ruling planets. Also the same are the Midheaven and Ascendant signs, but at different degrees, which illustrates how a relocation of even a relatively short distance can make a significant difference in an individual's life. Four planets change houses. These are the differences in his relocated chart:

- Pluto moves to the tenth house
- The Mars-Neptune-Venus stellium moves to the twelfth house
- Jupiter moves to conjunct the Ascendant
- The Moon moves to sextile the Midheaven

The Moon's sextile to the relocated Midheaven, an aspect that is not present in Clinton's birth chart, has much to do with his phenomenal popularity. The Moon represents the public, and the Midheaven represents his career and status.

With Jupiter conjunct the relocated Ascendant, he is able to personally (Ascendant) attract even more luck in Washington, D.C. This aspect also added to his popularity as president, but on the down side indicates that this location is one that could trigger weight gain because Jupiter is the planet of expansion. (After he left office, he had a visible weight loss.)

Pluto in the relocated tenth house boosts the strength and prominence of the Mercury-Saturn-Pluto stellium in Leo and is well suited to someone in such a powerful position. In this location, it is the only planet of the three that is sextile the Ascendant. Because Pluto

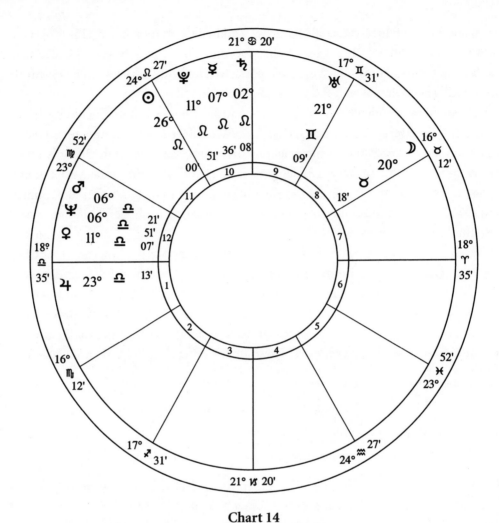

Chart 14
Bill Clinton, Chart Relocated to Washington, D.C.
August 19, 1946 / Washington, D.C. / 8:51 AM CST +6:00
Placidus Houses

also is the ruler of the birth and relocated second houses, Clinton could profit from the presidency, personally and financially, which he did. (He reportedly received a $10 million advance for his book, *My Life*, and has received high speaker fees, money he likely would not have seen had he not been president.)

Possibly the most fascinating feature in Clinton's relocated chart is the shift in the Ascendant that resulted in the Mars-Neptune-Venus stellium moving to the twelfth house of secrets and hidden matters. This clearly signifies the Monica Lewinsky affair, which, because of the stellium's square to the birth chart Midheaven, became public and was almost his undoing. Remember, these particular squares show potential for conflict, deceit, and trouble with women.

Aside from the fact that his wife, Hillary, wanted to be elected as a U.S. senator, which she did, the state of New York was an excellent post-White House choice for Clinton. His chart, when relocated to New York, a state almost directly north of Washington, D.C., is much the same. There is one major difference, however: The Sun is in the tenth house. He's thus likely to become even more popular in his "retirement." But the Mars-Neptune-Venus stellium remains in the relocated twelfth house, so he would be wise to be discreet.

Norman Schwarzkopf

General Norman Schwarzkopf achieved instant fame when he came to the attention of the public during the 1991 Gulf War. Dubbed "Stormin' Norman" during the conflict, the moniker accurately reflects his birth chart (chart 15).

Aries, the sign of the warrior, is on the Midheaven, which is squared by the aggressive, combative, fearless Mars-Pluto conjunction. Placed in Cancer (homeland, family), the conjunction also reflects his passionate patriotism. With Uranus conjunct the Midheaven, Schwarzkopf spots and seizes opportunities and revises his strategy to meet changing conditions—all with a unique, innovative approach.

The Leo Ascendant and Sun-Mercury conjunction give Schwarzkopf star presence, confidence, and leadership ability, and indicate that he's a dynamic speaker. Sun-Mercury in opposition to Saturn, an aspect combination that denotes brain power, also strengthens his tactical and analytical abilities and indicates he sets high standards for himself and others.

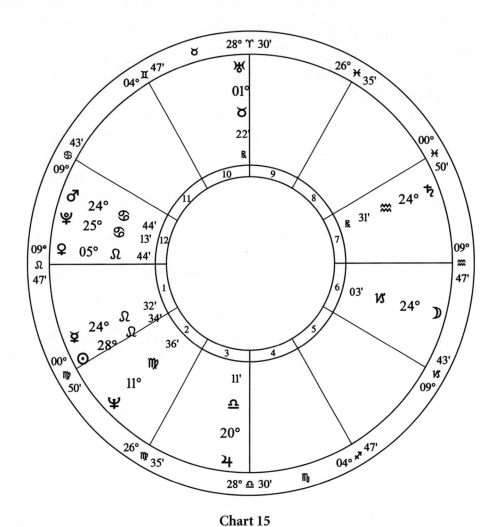

Chart 15
Norman Schwarzkopf, Birth Chart
August 22, 1934 / Trenton, NJ / 4:45 AM EDT +4:00
Placidus Houses

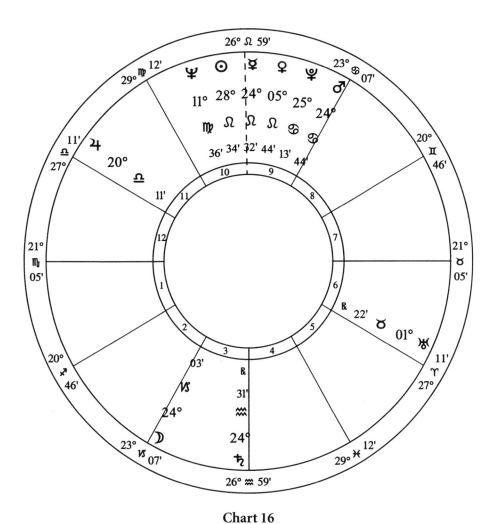

Chart 16
Norman Schwarzkopf, Chart Relocated to Al-Kuwayt, Kuwait
August 22, 1934 / Al-Kuwayt, Kuwait / 4:45 AM EDT +4:00
Placidus Houses

Fortunate, expansive Jupiter is part of a t-square that also includes Mars, Pluto, and the Moon. (A t-square is a major action-oriented chart configuration involving three or more planets, at least two of which are in opposition aspect and square a third.) In addition to intelligence, the t-square reinforces his ability to take charge and to plan and execute large-scale operations. With the Moon in Capricorn in the sixth house, he demands efficiency and responsibility from those under his command, and Jupiter in Libra accents fairness, justice, and people skills.

It's no surprise that Stormin' Norman claimed more than fifteen minutes of fame during the Gulf War. His chart relocated to Kuwait (chart 16) features seven planets above the horizon (Ascendant/Descendant axis), including Sun-Mercury conjunct the stellar Sun-ruled Leo Midheaven. Neptune in the tenth house created a romantic image in the public's mind, and enhanced his charm and charisma.

Steely, mysterious Scorpio on the relocated Ascendant adds a magnetic quality that gets an extra boost from Mars and Pluto trine/sextile the Ascendant/Descendant. The Moon sextile/trine the same axis from the third house favors communication and contact with the public, and the square from Sun-Mercury left no question about who was in charge. What the public didn't see, however, was the planning and strategy that went into the campaign and Schwarzkopf's extensive experience, all of which is symbolized by Saturn conjunct the IC.

These charts beautifully illustrate how even a temporary relocation can trigger career advancement and status by bringing the birth chart into focus where the individual can capitalize on the strengths, talents, and skills it represents.

Susan

In search of a new life, Susan (chart 17) took the plunge, loaded her car, and took off for Phoenix. As difficult as it was to leave her family, she knew intuitively that the time was right for a fresh start, especially on the heels of a second unsuccessful long-term relationship.

The desert Southwest had always intrigued her and she was ready for a warmer climate, having lived in Maine all her life. She had no job, but was confident she would find one and the career her ambitious Capricorn Ascendant had always wanted.

Mercury, ruler of the sixth house of work, opposite Saturn in the eighth house and square Uranus conjunct the Descendant reflects the unfulfilling, low-paying jobs Susan

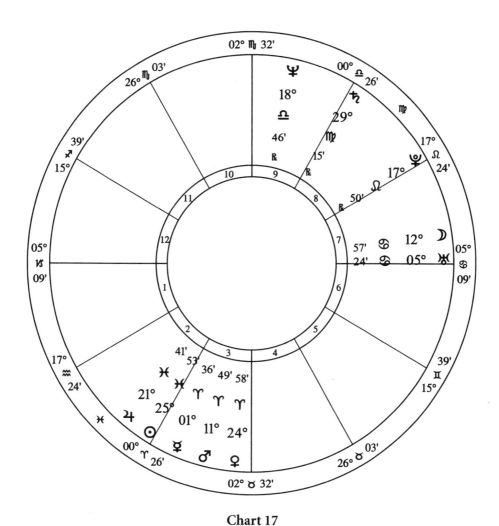

Chart 17
Susan, Birth Chart
March 17, 1951 / Lewiston, ME / 2:06 AM EST +5:00
Placidus Houses

held in Maine and her challenges with personal and working relationships. Yet with the Moon and Descendant in nurturing Cancer and the Sun in empathetic Pisces, people and family are a strong need. The Moon-Mars square also indicates highly emotional conflict with partners, and Venus opposite Neptune is an aspect of deception (self or others) and disillusionment.

With Uranus trine the Scorpio Midheaven, a career that offers independence and freedom of movement is important to her; she also could do well as an entrepreneur if she has the financial security the Capricorn Ascendant and Cancer Moon need. Her Midheaven ruler, Pluto, in the eighth house is trine Venus and Mars, so she has the potential to make money.

Within a week of Susan's arrival in Phoenix, she had a place to live and a job with the potential to become a career, which it ultimately did. Because she moved about 3,000 miles west of her birthplace, all the angles, house cusps, and planetary house placements, with the exception of Uranus, are different in the relocated chart (chart 18).

The fourth house is the most prominent in the relocated chart, with four planets (including the fortunate Sun-Jupiter conjunction) conjunct the relocated IC. Phoenix is definitely home to her, and the fourth house, which also is the house of beginnings, represents the fresh start she was looking for. Jupiter rules the adventuresome, extroverted Sagittarius Ascendant, giving her the ability to take a few more risks and expand her horizons.

The Virgo relocated Midheaven is comfortable energy for Susan because, like her birth chart Capricorn Ascendant, it's a practical earth sign. Saturn, which rules Capricorn, is in the tenth house, adding another layer of comfort to the chart, as well as a positive career outlet for her ambitions.

Relationships are more favorable with the relocated chart. Mercury, which rules the Midheaven and the Descendant, is sextile the Descendant, although still square Uranus, which is in the last degree of the seventh house. The Moon is sextile the Midheaven. With these placements, Susan has an opportunity to work through past relationship issues and emphasize the more positive indicators in her birth chart.

Careerwise, Susan accepted a job managing a retail landscape nursery and soon moved up to run the wholesale end of the business, where her income quadrupled. As a

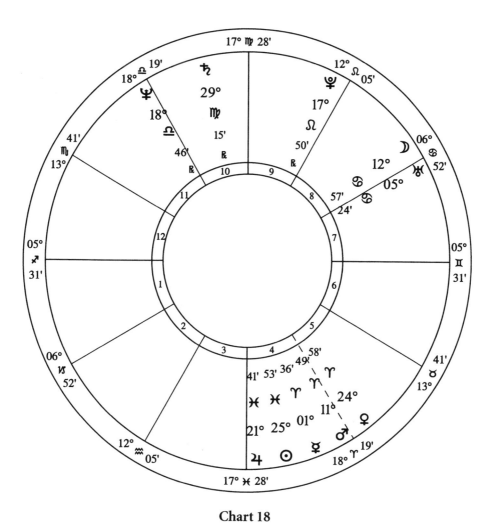

Chart 18
Susan, Chart Relocated to Phoenix, AZ
March 17, 1951 / Phoenix, AZ / 2:06 AM EST +5:00
Placidus Houses

result, she purchased a home, and felt secure enough to launch a home-based landscape design company while still maintaining the security of her day job. This is a positive use of the Mercury-Saturn opposition and the innovative Mercury-Uranus square as well as the fourth-house Sun-Jupiter conjunction. Her people skills and her caring Cancer Moon have been assets in both career endeavors.

1. David Maraniss quoted in "What Makes Clinton a Survivor?" by Richard Lacayo, *CNN.com*, September 21, 1998, http://www.cnn.com/ALLPOLITICS/time/1998/09/14/clinton.survivor.html.

2. Richard Lacayo, "What Makes Clinton a Survivor?," *CNN.com*, September 21, 1998, http://www.cnn.com/ALLPOLITICS/time/1998/09/14/clinton.survivor.html.

11
College

In the United States there are thousands of colleges, universities, community colleges, and vocational schools that offer degrees, certification, or specialized training and make higher education accessible to millions. Choosing the right location contributes to academic success as well as career success after college.

The more of these influences present in the relocated chart, the better:

- Mercury or Jupiter conjunct an angle
- Mercury, Jupiter, or Uranus sextile or trine an angle
- Mercury, Jupiter, or Uranus in or ruling the first, third, ninth, or eleventh house
- Planets in the third and/or ninth houses

Higher education can be expensive, so for many people, finances are an integral part of the college selection process. Scholarships and other grants are the first choice, because, unlike loans, they don't have to be repaid. Some students rely on help from parents or other family members, and others have full- or part-time jobs.

The following factors in the birth or relocated chart can help improve the odds for college funding:

- Venus conjunct, sextile, or trine an angle
- Jupiter in the eighth house
- Eighth-house ruler sextile or trine an angle

Chelsea Clinton

With an outgoing Leo Moon in the ninth house of higher education, Chelsea Clinton (chart 19) has a strong emotional investment in learning and pushes herself to shine; success in the classroom is a matter of pride. The Moon also rules the ninth house (with Cancer on the cusp).

Saturn, through Capricorn on the cusp, rules the third house of learning; and it is in Virgo in the tenth house of career. Chelsea therefore instinctively knows that education is a significant component of career success. Detail-oriented, analytical, practical Virgo reinforces her need to excel as a student (and later in her career), and she can be her own worst critic.

Saturn is opposite Mercury, the universal ruler of learning, and both planets square Neptune, forming a t-square. As already noted, a t-square is a major action-oriented planetary configuration. The planets and houses involved in the t-square represent a driving force in the individual's life. Resolution of the t-square, which comprises hard aspects—an opposition and two squares—comes through the house opposite the "t" planet; in Chelsea's chart it is the eighth house of other people's money. Chelsea is motivated to excel academically and to further her education as a career investment to achieve financial success.

The Mercury-Saturn opposition is an aspect of intelligence, and with Neptune in Sagittarius involved in the t-square, Chelsea is challenged to use creativity and vision to meet her goals. Because Mercury is in sensitive, intuitive Pisces, the sign ruled by Neptune, she can more easily tap into and successfully manage the t-square. Mercury trine Uranus also indicates intelligence, as well as an inventive mind, and with Uranus sextile Saturn, her thought process blends innovation and tradition.

Jupiter (the universal ruler of higher education) in the tenth house reinforces the importance of a college degree to career success, as does its conjunction to Mars, ruler of the sixth house of work through Aries. The high-energy Mars-Jupiter conjunction also signals an avid student, but with the planets in Virgo, she is relentless in her pursuit of academic perfection.

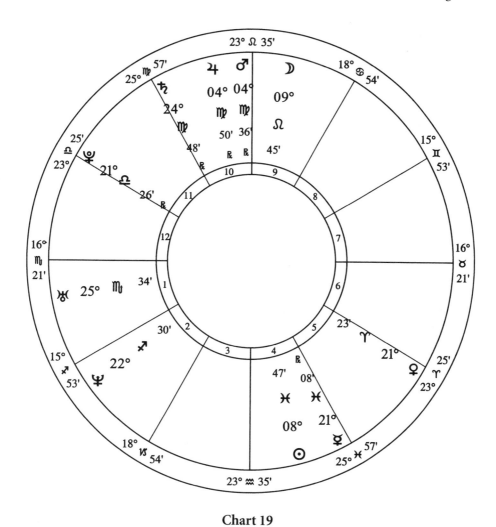

Chart 19
Chelsea Clinton, Birth Chart
February 27, 1980 / Little Rock, AR / 11:24 PM CST +6:00
Placidus Houses

Chelsea enrolled in Stanford University while her father, President Bill Clinton, was in office, and four years later she earned a degree in history. These are the changes in Chelsea's chart relocated to Palo Alto, California (chart 20):

- Ascendant changes from Scorpio to Libra
- Midheaven changes from Leo to Cancer
- All house cusps change signs
- All planets change houses

Chelsea's parents effectively shielded her from the media and the public during their White House years, in part so she would have as normal a childhood as possible, given the circumstances. This makes the relocated chart particularly fascinating.

With the natal Ascendant shift from hidden, reserved Scorpio (which it also is in her chart relocated to Washington, D.C.) to people-oriented Libra, Chelsea "emerged" into the world. The same is true of the Moon, which rules the public; it moves to the tenth house, and the sign it rules, Cancer, is on the Midheaven. The relocated chart also features Libra's ruling planet, Venus, conjunct the Descendant, adding further to the emphasis on other people and developing relationships in the wider world, as does the Mars-Jupiter conjunction and Saturn in the eleventh house of friendship.

Chelsea's college choice gave her several advantages for academic success. Mercury and Uranus (trine in her birth chart) are trine/sextile the relocated Midheaven/IC axis. Mercury rules the relocated ninth house, and Jupiter rules the relocated third, where Neptune is placed, offering an opportunity to use the practical creativity of the t-square. Pluto conjunct the Ascendant adds determination, and its square to the Midheaven indicates the tremendous pressure she felt to succeed.

Mercury and Uranus in aspect to the angles reinforces communication, writing, logic, and independence, and this location is an excellent one to maximize the intelligence of the natal trine. So, while the birth chart t-square also aspects the relocated Midheaven/IC through Mercury, this location emphasizes the trine. She might have had some difficulty had Saturn, for example, been conjunct one of the angles.

Had Chelsea been a less motivated student, however, this relocated chart could have presented a challenge with socializing versus study time. The Sun and Mercury in the fifth house and Mars and Jupiter in the eleventh emphasize socializing, dating, group activities, fun, and recreation, which some college students carry to excess. Saturn in the

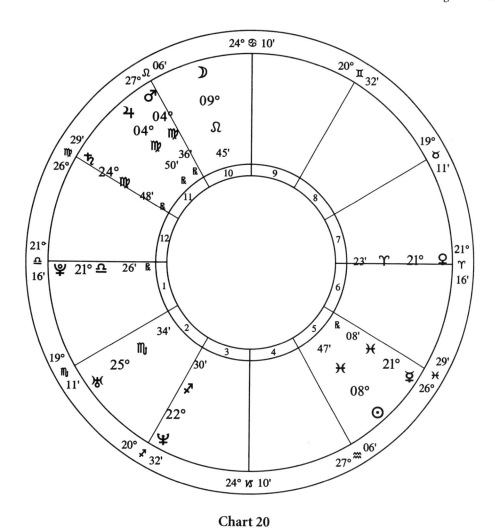

Chart 20

Chelsea Clinton, Chart Relocated to Palo Alto, CA

February 27, 1980 / Palo Alto, CA / 11:24 PM CST +6:00

Placidus Houses

eleventh house and sextile the relocated Midheaven, however, adds a responsible influence and is a reminder of the long-term goals associated with the t-square. Venus conjunct the relocated Descendant and square the relocated Midheaven also puts socializing in focus in this location.

Taken as a whole, this college location was a good one for Chelsea, an excellent student who obviously had her priorities in perspective because she went on to earn a master's degree in international relations at Oxford University in England. In that location, Mercury in the first house is trine the relocated Midheaven, which is conjunct ninth-house Uranus.

Karl

Karl applied to and visited many colleges and universities before deciding on the University of Virginia, a school known for its high academic standards and selective admissions process. His intention from the outset was to earn a bachelor's degree and then enter medical school.

Karl's quick, intelligent, penetrating mind is evident in his birth chart (chart 21). Three planets in the third house of learning and in Libra, a mentally oriented air sign, reflect curiosity and a thirst for information. This influence, combined with Mercury square Pluto, indicates persistence, determination, and problem-solving ability. Research skills are a strength, and he probes deeply and with an intense focus that helps him master the subject. He's a quick study, with Mars square the Saturn-Jupiter conjunction, and able to sift through a large volume of material to capture the important points. But he overdoes it at times and should schedule regular breaks to prevent frustration and burnout. The twelfth-house Sun sextile Saturn also increases his ability to tune out the world and concentrate.

Karl's relocated chart (chart 22) is similar to his birth chart. The Ascendant and Midheaven signs are the same, as are the house cusp signs. Although only three planets change houses, the shift is significant. The chart reflects the potential for a healthy blend of academic, social, and campus activities, all of which he knew were necessary for later admittance to medical school.

Although the Moon does not change houses, it shifts to a conjunction with the Midheaven, giving him the edge to become involved and well-known on campus. Mercury in the relocated eleventh house adds emphasis to clubs, organizations, and friendships,

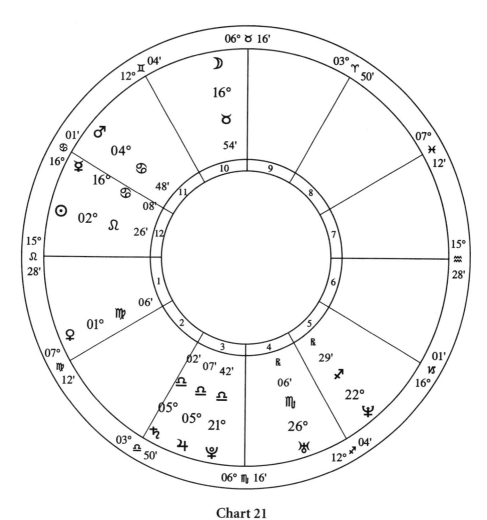

Chart 21
Karl, Birth Chart
July 25, 1981 / Indianapolis, IN / 6:48 AM EST +5:00
Placidus Houses

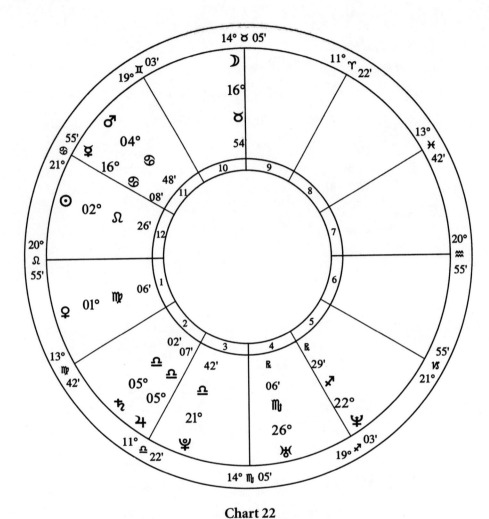

Chart 22

Karl, Chart Relocated to Charlottesville, VA

July 25, 1981 / Charlottesville, VA / 6:48 AM EST +5:00

Placidus Houses

and its sextile to the Midheaven is beneficial for education. The Ascendant increases by about 6° in the relocated chart, so Neptune moves into a closer trine to it, highlighting romance and socializing.

Saturn and Jupiter change houses from the third to the second, somewhat easing the intense academic pressure of the birth chart influence. Pluto, besides remaining in the third house and in square aspect to Mercury (now in the eleventh house of goals), moves into a close sextile to the Ascendant. This influence was therefore strong enough to keep him motivated and on task, adding willpower and determination.

Karl planned ahead and designed his undergraduate years to achieve his goal to attend medical school. After considering several locations, he decided to return to his birthplace and enrolled at Indiana University. The chart for this college experience is therefore the same as his birth chart.

He could have chosen a school on the East Coast, which would have been similar to the relocated chart for his undergraduate years, or one on the West Coast, with Mercury conjunct the relocated Ascendant. When all factors are considered, however, having three planets in the third house, including Jupiter, and Mercury in the twelfth, is an asset for the intensity and volume of work involved and the concentration required to earn a medical degree. He is in his second year and doing well.

12
Money

Money motivates, especially in a materialistic society. The perception that more is better encourages people to live on credit and take risks. Although relocation can improve your financial prospects, this is an area of life that requires a careful assessment of birth chart potential. Remember, the birth chart is still the birth chart; relocation only changes the emphasis.

Relocation can increase the financial gain promised in a birth chart and improve difficult planetary placements. It also can encourage free spending, unwise speculation, or a miserly attitude.

These influences in a relocated chart can benefit money matters:

- Venus conjunct, sextile, or trine an angle
- Venus in the second or eighth house
- Jupiter in the second or eighth house
- Second-house ruler or co-ruler in the second house or sextile or trine an angle
- Eighth-house ruler or co-ruler in the second house
- Second-house ruler or co-ruler in the eighth house
- Second- and eighth-house rulers or co-rulers sextile or trine each other

Jack Nicholson

A ten-time Oscar nominee and three-time winner, Jack Nicholson is known for his stunning performances in such films as *Easy Rider, Chinatown, Terms of Endearment, One Flew Over the Cuckoo's Nest, The Witches of Eastwick,* and *As Good as It Gets.*

Nicholson got his start in Hollywood as an office boy in MGM's cartoon department. He studied acting on the side, and today his wealth is estimated to be $150 million.

Moneymaking potential exists in Nicholson's birth chart (chart 23), but also the potential for sizable losses. Career earnings are the most likely source of money in this chart, which has the Sun (second-house ruler) conjunct Uranus (eighth-house ruler) in the tenth house. With Uranus (planet of the unexpected) involved, this aspect signals sudden financial reversals, windfalls, and debt.

The other significant aspect pattern is a t-square involving Venus, Jupiter, and Pluto. The planets and houses involved in the t-square represent friction and obstacles, but the t-square also signifies action. The individual can therefore use the energy to achieve a goal, resolve a situation, or retreat. With a determined Taurus Sun and a dramatic Leo Ascendant (both fixed signs), Nicholson is more likely to persist and face conflict head-on than to back down.

With money planet Venus, expansive Jupiter, and transformative Pluto in the t-square, he nevertheless could easily have ended up penniless. This configuration is one of boom or bust, and it is directed into career (tenth house), job/working conditions (sixth house), and behind-the-scenes activities or hidden matters (twelfth house).

The tenth-house Mercury trine Neptune in the second house accents income through creative careers. Illusive Neptune, universal ruler of cinema, is prominent in the charts of many successful actors.

Luck was on Nicholson's side when he moved to Los Angeles. There, his relocated chart (chart 24) emphasizes the positive and minimizes the negative as much as is possible within the continental United States. Here are the changes in the relocated chart:

- Leo Ascendant changes to Gemini
- Aries Midheaven changes to Aquarius
- All house cusps change signs
- All planets change houses

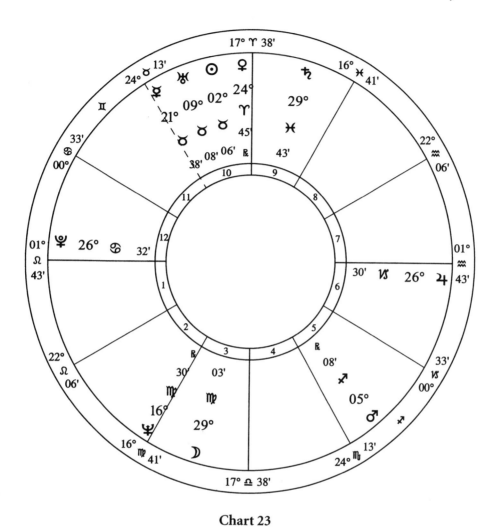

Chart 23
Jack Nicholson, Birth Chart
April 22, 1937 / Neptune, NJ / 11:00 AM EST +5:00
Placidus Houses

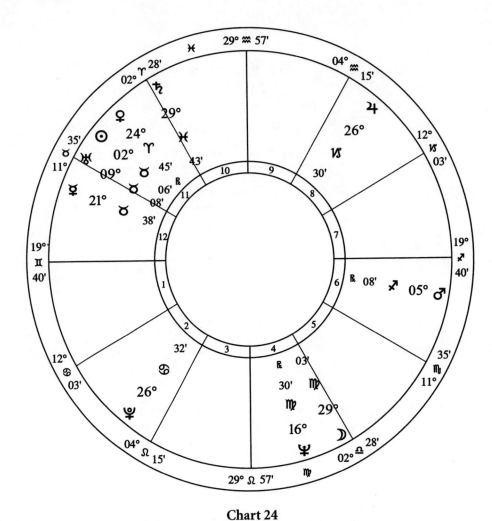

Chart 24
Jack Nicholson, Chart Relocated to Los Angeles, CA
April 22, 1937 / Los Angeles, CA / 11:00 AM EST +5:00
Placidus Houses

The Midheaven sign switches from Aries to Aquarius, ruled by Uranus. This gives him more of the benefit of the opportunistic Sun-Uranus conjunction without the extreme career volatility suggested by its tenth-house natal placement.

The Ascendant shifts from Leo to Gemini to combine extroversion and a more light-hearted approach, which is an added plus for an entertainer. Because Mercury rules Gemini, Nicholson can more easily tap into the creative and intuitive energy of the Mercury-Neptune trine.

In his relocated chart, Venus is in the eleventh house, with the Pluto-Jupiter opposition spanning the second/eighth houses of money—an improvement, or not? Because Venus is sextile rather than conjunct the Midheaven in this location, the t-square is softened somewhat, providing Nicholson the opportunity to plan and make informed financial and career decisions rather than immediately responding to events.

But the relocated chart presents a potential stumbling block of another sort: the Moon and Saturn, which rule the second and eighth houses, are in opposition. This aspect is one associated with austerity-thinking, and can indicate miserliness. Security issues are the root cause, and many individuals with this aspect never reach a personal financial comfort zone. Could that be one reason Nicholson is a millionaire 150 times over?

Sue Grafton

Author Sue Grafton is best known for her series of mystery novels that feature private investigator Kinsey Millhone. Each title features a letter of the alphabet—*A Is for Alibi*, *B Is for Burglar*, *C Is for Corpse*, etc.—and they have been published in twenty-eight countries and twenty-six languages.

She worked as a Hollywood screenwriter for fifteen years, a job she disliked, but one that she says polished her writing skills. When Grafton found herself in the middle of a bitter divorce, she says she would "lie in bed at night just thinking of ways to do him in."[1] Those thoughts became the plot for her first alphabet series book.

Grafton's birth chart (chart 25) shows good earning potential, including the Sun in Taurus, a sign that attracts money and strives for financial security. Second-house ruler Venus in the third house of communication is sextile Jupiter and conjunct Mars, which is sextile Mercury (writing). This Gemini-Aries alignment indicates moneymaking ideas, initiative, and energy, and its tendency to spend impulsively and scatter resources

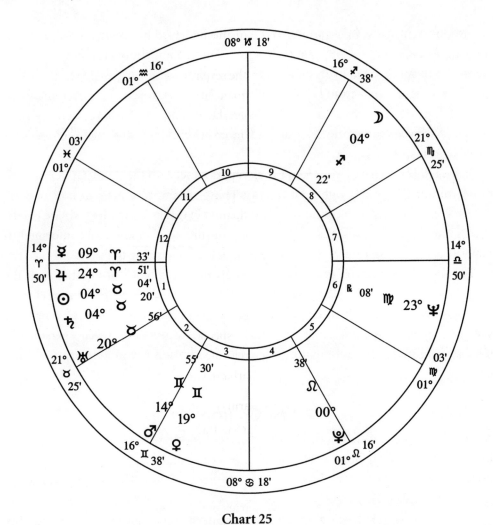

Chart 25
Sue Grafton, Birth Chart
April 24, 1940 / Louisville, KY / 4:10 AM CST +6:00
Placidus Houses

is minimized by the thrifty Sun-Saturn conjunction. Mars also co-rules the eighth house through Scorpio.

With Venus ruling the second house and the seventh house (partnership), this planet's square to Neptune shows the possibility for financial and/or romantic deception and disillusionment. Grafton was twice divorced when she met author Steven Humphrey, whom she married in 1978. She obviously uses the more positive, inspirational, creative energy of this aspect in her writing.

The eighth-house Moon in Sagittarius is part of a grand trine that includes Pluto, which rules the eighth house, and Mercury. This gives Grafton the potential to earn a sizable income in the communications field, and even more so when working behind the scenes (twelfth-house Mercury) at home (fourth-house Pluto). People with a Sun-Saturn conjunction are often content with their own company and thus work well on their own in solitude; she probably prefers this because Mercury is square the Midheaven and Sun-Saturn is trine it.

When a birth chart shows the financial potential that Grafton's does, the right location can enhance and help fulfill it. This is especially true when the most promising source of income is also highlighted in the relocated chart. These are the changes when Grafton's birth chart is relocated to Santa Barbara, California, where she currently lives:

- Ascendant changes from Aries to Aquarius
- Midheaven changes from Capricorn to Sagittarius
- All house cusps change signs
- All planets change houses

The Ascendant switches from Aries to Aquarius in Grafton's relocated chart (chart 26). Besides the obvious benefit an air sign (mental, intellectual) has for a writer, independent Aquarius is a fixed sign, which provides the follow-through that Aries lacks. Sagittarius, the relocated Midheaven sign, is adventuresome, unlike the conservative Capricorn Midheaven in her birth chart; Sagittarius also rules the publishing industry.

Mercury, always an important career indicator in a writer's chart, is trine the relocated Midheaven from the second house; it is square the birth chart Midheaven. The relocation shifts the Mars-Venus conjunction to the fourth house, with Mercury ruling the relocated (Gemini) IC and Mars, which is sextile Mercury, ruling the relocated second

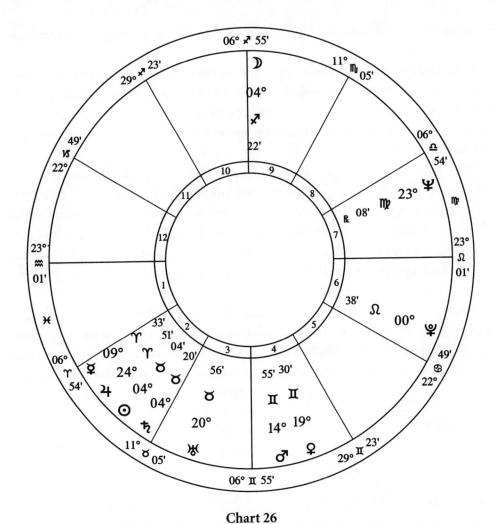

Chart 26
Sue Grafton, Chart Relocated to Santa Barbara, CA
April 24, 1940 / Santa Barbara, CA / 4:10 AM CST +6:00
Placidus Houses

house. In this location, Grafton can then make money as a writer who works from home.

The grand trine becomes more prominent in the relocated chart. The Moon, which rules the public, rises to the highest point in the chart, conjunct the Midheaven from the ninth house of publishing. Mercury shifts from the hidden twelfth house to the second house of money, and Pluto is in the sixth house of work and the ruler of the ninth.

Venus switches its rulership from the birth chart second house and seventh (partnership) house to the relocated third (writing) and eighth houses, further reinforcing this location as one in which Grafton can make money writing at home. Also favorable is Venus' sextile to Jupiter, now in the second house and sextile/trine the Ascendant/Descendant. Jupiter rules the relocated Sagittarius Midheaven.

The Venus-Neptune square shifts from the third and sixth houses to the fourth and seventh, where the aspect retains its birth chart emphasis on money, communication, and partnership (birth chart Venus in the third house and ruling the second and seventh). But with Leo on the relocated Descendant, the Sun, its ruler, becomes more influential in relationships. Therefore, so does the steadying effect of the practical Sun-Saturn conjunction, which indicates karma, life lessons, and the potential for a long-term union, possibly with a soul mate. On the down side, the relocated first-house ruler, Uranus, square the Ascendant/Descendant suggests a sudden change in a relationship, which occurred in Grafton's life. As is typical of Uranus, however, the unexpected included a flash of insight that launched a new career.

Relocated Uranus would trine/sextile the Midheaven/IC axis in locations from central North Dakota south through the western third of Texas. But such a relocated chart would have a Pisces Ascendant, with its ruler, Neptune, conjunct the Descendant and square Venus in the third house—a similar influence (but a stronger one, because of the Descendant conjunction) to that in the Santa Barbara relocated chart. Careerwise, the eastern locations feature Jupiter trine/sextile the Midheaven/IC, but Mars-Venus is square the Ascendant/Descendant, and Mercury aspects no angle.

Whether by instinct, astrology, or luck, and when all factors are considered, Sue Grafton made a smart choice when she set up shop in California.

---

1. Linda Richards, "'G' Is for Grafton," *January Magazine*, http://www.januarymagazine.com/grafton.html.

13
Recreation and Retirement

Recreation and retirement share the common goals of relaxation, free time, exploring new horizons or delving more deeply into familiar ones, and simply enjoying life. The main difference is the time frame: a one- or two-week vacation versus 365 days a year to call your own.

Travel is a favorite leisure-time pursuit, and many people choose to relocate upon retirement. Finding the right vacation location is, of course, far less risky than leaving familiar territory behind and committing to a long-distance move. This is one reason to shop around for a retirement spot by vacationing or spending several months in various locations. Narrowing the choices is easier with the help of a relocated chart, but it's up to you to first define what you want. What interests one person may be boring to another.

The following are some general guidelines to use when exploring vacation and retirement possibilities.

Family Life

- Several planets in the fourth house
- Moon conjunct, sextile, or trine the IC

- Fourth-house ruler or co-ruler conjunct, sextile, or trine an angle
- Fourth-house ruler or co-ruler in the fourth house

Health Enhancement

- Mars sextile or trine an angle
- Sixth-house ruler or co-ruler sextile or trine an angle
- Sun, Mars, or Jupiter in the first house
- Sun, Mars, or Jupiter sextile or trine the sixth-house ruler or co-ruler

Hobbies and Creative Activities

- Several planets in the fifth house, or a fifth-house planet trine the Ascendant
- Sun, Mars, Venus, or Neptune in the fifth house
- Sun conjunct, sextile, or trine an angle
- Fifth-house ruler or co-ruler in the fifth house or sextile or trine a planet in the fifth house
- Fifth house ruler or co-ruler conjunct, sextile, or trine the Ascendant or Midheaven

Part-time or Consulting Work

- Planets in the sixth house
- Sixth-house planet(s) trine the Midheaven
- Sixth-house ruler or co-ruler conjunct, trine, or sextile the Midheaven

Travel

- Planets in the ninth or third house
- Jupiter or Mercury conjunct, sextile, or trine an angle
- Jupiter or Mercury in the ninth or third house

Friendship and Group Activities

- Planets in the eleventh house
- Uranus sextile or trine an angle, especially the Ascendant
- Eleventh-house ruler or co-ruler sextile the Ascendant
- Eleventh-house ruler or co-ruler in the eleventh house
- Eleventh house ruler or co-ruler conjunct, sextile, or trine an eleventh-house planet

Mental Stimulation

- Planets in the third or ninth house
- Mercury conjunct, sextile, or trine an angle
- Third- or ninth-house ruler or co-ruler conjunct, sextile, or trine the Ascendant or a planet in the third or ninth house
- Third-house planet sextile the Ascendant
- Ninth-house planet trine the Ascendant

Hal and Linda

Choosing a retirement location was simple for Hal, an engineer, and Linda, a teacher. They moved to Phoenix to live near their only child, a son who had relocated to the area several years before. Because of previous visits with him, they were somewhat familiar with the city and climate.

Their retirement goals were well-defined: Hal wanted to indulge his passion for learning and lifelong quest for knowledge by filling his days studying history, researching his family tree and esoteric subjects, and other scholarly pursuits. For Linda, days filled with friendship, club and organization activities, homemaking, and crafts projects would be the ideal. Phoenix has fulfilled their needs and expectations.

Hal's relocated chart (chart 27) has an Aquarius Ascendant, with the ruler, Uranus, in the first house. This air sign and planet of independence have a liberating effect, providing the freedom to explore his interests. With Neptune conjunct the Leo Descendant, and the Sun (Descendant ruler) conjunct Venus in Libra, sign of relationships, the relocated chart reinforces the couple's loving, romantic ties.

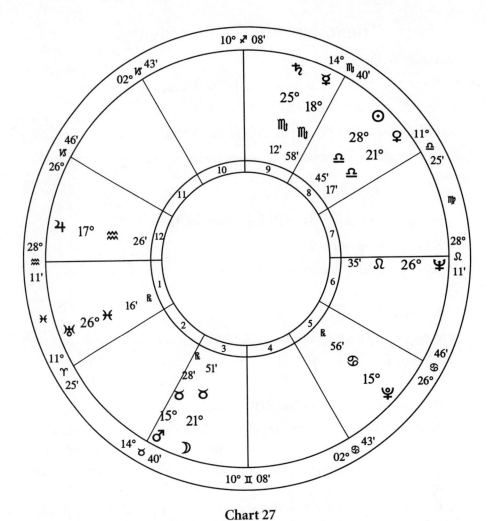

Chart 27
Hal, Chart Relocated to Phoenix, AZ
October 22, 1926 / Phoenix, AZ / 4:00 PM CST +6:00
Placidus Houses

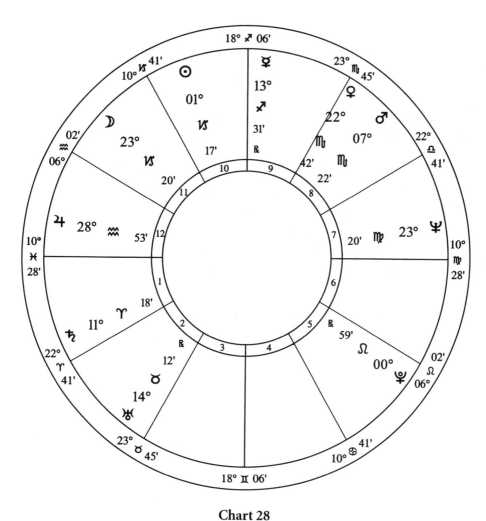

Chart 28
Linda, Chart Relocated to Phoenix, AZ
December 23, 1938 / Phoenix, AZ / 1:30 PM EST +5:00
Placidus Houses

Prominent in Hal's relocated chart is the ninth-house Mercury-Saturn conjunction in Scorpio, the sign of research. The ninth is the house of knowledge, and Mercury is the planet of learning. The third house of learning and information also is emphasized with a Moon-Mars conjunction in pleasure-loving Taurus, a sign that is patient and thorough and complements the depth of the ninth-house Scorpio. Moon-Mars is sextile Pluto, ruler of the ninth house, which is trine Mercury. The first-house Uranus also is trine Mercury-Saturn.

The Sun-Venus conjunction in the eighth house is financially beneficial and a positive influence for a comfortable income.

Linda's relocated chart (chart 28) also shows her desires being fulfilled in Phoenix. Saturn, ruler of the eleventh house of friendship and group activities, is in the first house. The Moon, which rules the fifth house of recreation, creativity, and hobbies, is in the eleventh, so she combines the two interests.

Neptune, which rules the Pisces Ascendant, is in the seventh house of relationships, so much of her focus is on other people, friends, loved ones, and Hal. She enjoys being with others, and, with the Sun in the tenth house and ruling the sixth, she's popular and a hard worker in clubs and organizations.

Mercury, through Gemini, rules the IC in both relocated charts, so communication and a high level of activity are the norm in their home. Hal spends his days in his home study, and Linda reads and learns new cooking and hobby techniques with her ninth-house Mercury in wisdom-seeking Sagittarius trine Saturn in the first house.

Linda's chart, however, shows the potential for financial tension because of Venus and Mars in the eighth house in opposition to Uranus in the second house. This indicates unexpected expenses, fluctuating income, and buying on impulse, which can increase debt. Fortunately, the couple is aware of this, and Hal handles the day-to-day finances.

Mike and Marianne

Although Mike and Marianne have vacationed in many locations, their first choice is San Diego, California. They have returned there year after year to enjoy the temperate climate, ocean, and historic and cultural sites in and around the city.

San Diego feels like home to Mike, whose relocated chart (chart 29) has four planets in the fourth house, including Venus, which rules the fifth house of recreation. Sagittar-

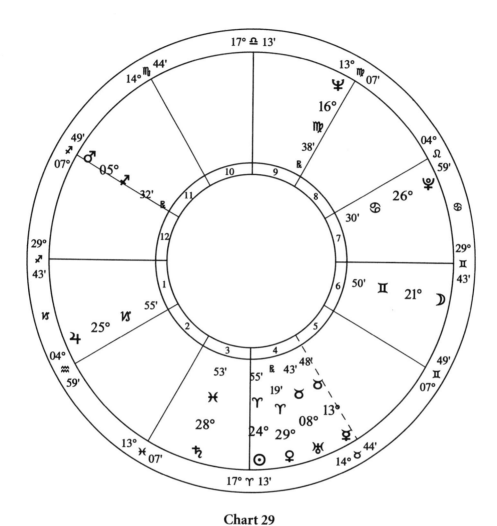

Chart 29
Mike, Chart Relocated to San Diego, CA
April 15, 1937 / San Diego, CA / 2:20 AM EST +5:00
Placidus Houses

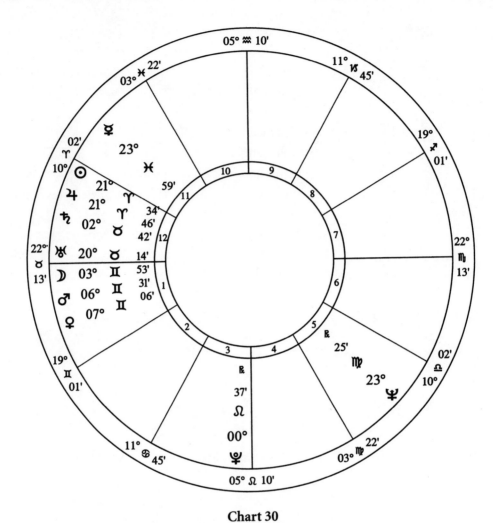

Chart 30
Marianne, Chart Relocated to San Diego, CA
April 11, 1940 / San Diego, CA / 10:00 AM EST +5:00
Placidus Houses

ius, sign of travel and adventure as well as knowledge, is on the Ascendant, and its ruler, Jupiter, is in the first house.

Neptune, the universal ruler of water, is in the ninth house of travel and trine ninth-house ruler Mercury in the fourth house. Neptune in the ninth house also accents this location as a sanctuary, a place to get away from the daily grind. Mercury ruling the Descendant and trine Neptune favors romance.

San Diego is even more of a symbolic sanctuary for Marianne, whose relocated chart (chart 30) has four planets in the twelfth house and Neptune (water) in the fifth. With Taurus on the Ascendant, this location invites indulgence in the sensual pleasures of life, including good food and a slower pace.

Yet the first-house Gemini Moon conjunct Mars and Venus makes informal learning and sightseeing fun, especially in the company of her husband. The stellium strengthens communication in this location, as does Pluto in the third house, and here the couple can take the time to discuss mutual concerns in a more relaxed setting.

Appendix 1
Goals and Locations

If you want to achieve a specific goal through relocation, start with the goal and check the list below. The more influences—aspects to the angles, house placements, ruling planets—you have in a geographic area, the more successful you're likely to be in meeting your goal.

Artistic ability: Venus conjunction the Descendant, Ascendant, Midheaven, or IC; Venus or Neptune sextile or trine any angle. Venus or Neptune in the first or fifth house (more personal focus) or in the second, sixth, or tenth house (more professional focus).

Astrology (emphasis on): Uranus conjunction, opposition, sextile, or trine the Ascendant or Midheaven.

Beauty (physical): Venus and/or Neptune conjunction, sextile, or trine the Ascendant, or in the first house.

Career development: Saturn sextile or trine the Midheaven. Several planets in the tenth house. Jupiter conjunction, sextile, or trine the Midheaven. Pluto sextile or trine the

Midheaven. The Sun conjunction, sextile, or trine the Midheaven. Any planet ruling the Midheaven making a sextile or trine to the Midheaven.

Children: Several planets in the fifth house. The fifth-house ruler or co-ruler conjunction, sextile, or trine an angle. The Sun or Moon in the fifth house. The Moon or Sun conjunction, sextile, or trine the fifth-house ruler or co-ruler.

Communication/media: Mercury conjunction, sextile or trine an angle. Mercury in the first or third house (personal emphasis) or in the second, sixth, or tenth house (professional emphasis). Several planets in the third house.

Creativity: The Sun conjunction, sextile, or trine an angle. The Sun in the first or fifth house. The Sun, Mars, Venus, or Mercury conjunction, sextile, or trine the ruler or co-ruler of the fifth house. Any planet in the fifth house trine the Ascendant. The ruler or co-ruler of the fifth house conjunction the Ascendant or Midheaven, or sextile or trine any planet in the fifth house.

Diplomacy/empathy/negotiating skills: Venus conjunction, sextile, or trine an angle or in the seventh house. The planet ruling the seventh house conjunction, sextile, or trine an angle or in the first or seventh house.

Energy/vitality: Mars and/or the Sun and/or Jupiter conjunction, sextile, or trine an angle. Mars, the Sun, or Jupiter in the first house.

Faith (strengthen): Jupiter conjunction, sextile, or trine an angle, or in the first, ninth, or twelfth house.

Financial gain: Venus conjunction, sextile, or trine an angle. Venus in the second house. The planet ruling the second house in the second house and/or sextile or trine an angle (especially the Midheaven). Jupiter in the second house. The ruler or co-ruler of the eighth house in the second house. A sextile or trine between the rulers or co-rulers of the second and eighth houses.

Friendship: Uranus sextile or trine an angle. Uranus in the eleventh house. The planet ruling the eleventh house conjunction, sextile, or trine an angle. Several planets in the eleventh house.

Health enhancement: Mars sextile or trine an angle. The planet ruling the sixth house sextile or trine an angle. Mars, the Sun, or Jupiter in the first house or sextile or trine the ruler or co-ruler of the sixth house.

Home/family emphasis: The Moon conjunction, sextile, or trine an angle (especially the IC). Several planets in the fourth house. The ruler or co-ruler of the fourth house conjunction, sextile, or trine an angle.

Independence: Mars, Jupiter, and/or Uranus conjunction, sextile, or trine an angle or in the first, ninth, or eleventh house.

Love: Venus, the Sun, or the Moon conjunction, sextile, or trine an angle (especially the Ascendant, Descendant, or IC). A sextile or trine between the rulers or co-rulers of the fifth, seventh, and eighth houses, or between the rulers or co-rulers of these houses and the Sun, the Moon, or Venus.

Marriage/partnership: Venus conjunction, sextile, or trine an angle. The planet ruling the seventh house conjunction, sextile, or trine an angle. Several planets in the seventh house. The ruler or co-ruler of the seventh house sextile or trine Venus or planet(s) in the seventh house.

Mental stimulation/education: Mercury or Jupiter conjunction an angle. Mercury, Jupiter, or Uranus sextile or trine an angle. Mercury, Jupiter, or Uranus in the first, third, ninth, or eleventh house. Several planets in the third or ninth house.

Pleasure/gratification: Venus conjunction, sextile, or trine an angle. Venus in the first or second house.

Productivity: Mercury and/or Saturn in the second, sixth, or tenth house, or conjunction the Midheaven, or sextile or trine another angle. The planets ruling the sixth and tenth houses conjunction, sextile, or trine an angle.

Research skills: Pluto and/or Saturn sextile or trine an angle. Pluto or Saturn in the sixth, eighth, or tenth house.

Resolute/steadfast: Pluto and/or Saturn sextile or trine an angle. Pluto or Saturn in the first house.

Romance: The Sun and/or Venus conjunction, sextile, or trine an angle. The planet ruling the fifth house conjunction, sextile, or trine an angle. Several planets in the fifth house.

Sanctuary: Neptune sextile or trine an angle. Neptune in the twelfth or fourth house.

Sexuality in focus: Mars, Pluto, and/or the Sun sextile or trine an angle, or in the second, fifth, or eighth house. Several planets in the fifth or eighth house.

Spiritual emphasis: Jupiter and/or Neptune conjunction, sextile, or trine an angle. Neptune or Jupiter in the ninth or twelfth house.

Sports activity: Mars and/or Jupiter conjunction, sextile, or trine an angle. Mars and/or Jupiter in the first, fifth, or ninth house.

Status (increased): Saturn and Jupiter in the tenth house. Saturn sextile or trine an angle. Jupiter conjunction the Midheaven, or sextile or trine an angle. The Sun conjunction, sextile, or trine the Midheaven.

Travel: Jupiter and/or Mercury conjunction, sextile, or trine an angle. Jupiter or Mercury in the ninth, third, or first house. Several planets in the third or ninth house.

Appendix 2
Map Your Travels & Relocation
Using the CD-ROM

First you need to install the program. Just remove the CD-ROM from its folder and place it in your computer's CD-ROM drive. The program will begin to install itself.

If it does not start automatically, click on the Start menu and select "Run." In the Run menu dialog box, type in your corresponding CD-ROM drive followed by the file name SETUP.exe. Typically, the CD-ROM is set up as D:\. The install wizard will run and guide you through the rest of the process.

For an alternate method, you can access your CD-ROM drive by clicking on "My Computer" and then the CD-ROM drive (typically D:\). Double-click on the SETUP.exe icon.

When you double-click on the program icon, you will see a screen called "Mapping Your Travels & Relocation," which is pictured on the following page.

Mapping Your Travels & Relocation is a basic astrology program, designed around the most sophisticated astrology programming available. Cosmic Patterns, in collaboration with Llewellyn Worldwide, has developed this program to provide you with birth charts (the circle with all the astrological symbols) and charts relocated to cities of your choice. The program also provides basic interpretations of those charts (six- to seven-page printouts of information about the location).

Let's discuss the choices you have on this screen:

- The Start menu is used to create a chart.
- The About menu provides information about Llewellyn Worldwide, the publisher of *Mapping Your Travels & Relocation,* and Cosmic Patterns Software, the designer of the program.
- The Quit menu allows you to exit the program.

Creating an Astrology Chart and Relocation Interpretation

To use your program, click on the Start menu at the top of the screen and select "New List of Charts (New Session)." If you are returning to the program and want to see the last chart you made, select "Continue with Charts of Previous Session."

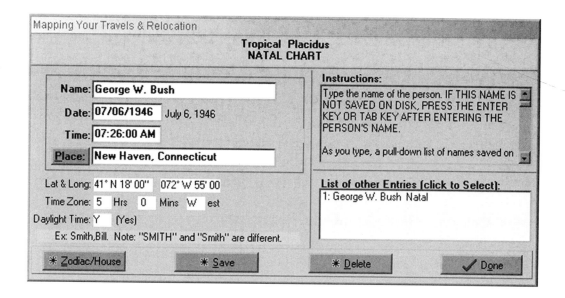

This is where you enter your birth information. There are some simple instructions on the right side of the screen, similar to what follows here. Let's make a birth chart for George W. Bush as an example. He was born on July 6, 1946, at 7:26 AM in New Haven, Connecticut.

- In the Name box, type "George W. Bush," and Enter.

- In the Date box, type "07061946", and Enter. (Always enter the date in mm dd yyyy format.)

- In the Time field, type "072600 AM" (the birth time in hh mm ss format), and Enter.

- In the Place box, type "New Haven, Connecticut" (the birthplace). As soon as you type the word "New," a list will drop down. You can continue typing, or look for New Haven, Connecticut in this list by clicking repeatedly on the down arrow.

You can go back up by clicking on the up arrow. You will see some places you have probably never heard of, but you will come to New Haven, Connecticut. Select it. The drop-down list will disappear, and you will see New Haven, Connecticut in the Place box. You will also see information filled in the boxes below it: the latitude is 41N18 00, the longitude is 072W55 00, the time zone is 5 hours 0 minutes West, and the Daylight Saving Time box is marked "Y."

If your city does not automatically come up in the list, you can use a nearby city from the list. You can also look up your birthplace in an atlas to find the latitude and longitude, time zone, and daylight saving time information, and fill in this information. Generally, a city close to the birthplace is close enough for most purposes and will also be in the same time zone. If the time zone information is different, your chart could be off by an hour one way or the other. Your chart will be slightly different depending on the distance your choice is from your actual birthplace. You can obtain the correct longitude, latitude, and time information from a timetable book for astrology.[1]

The Zodiac/House button allows you to select a different house system. This program automatically selects the tropical zodiac and the Placidus house system. Experiment with the other choices to see what changes on the chart wheel. In this program the interpretation will change only if you select the sidereal zodiac.

Select the "Save" button at the bottom of the screen to save the chart (you can delete it later if you need to), and then click "OK."

Then select the "Done" button. If you forget to save and go directly to the Done button, you will get a prompt asking if you want to save the data. In fact, all the way along prompts appear to help you enter the data.

A window will appear with a list of places. You can choose a relocation city from this list by highlighting a city, or you can begin typing the relocation city into the space at the top of the list. As you type, the list will move to that point alphabetically in the list, and you can choose from the list or continue typing. If your location does not appear in the list, choose a city close to your desired location.

The screen pictured on the next page is what you will see next.

---

1. Here are two possibilities: *The American Atlas*, compiled and programmed by Neil F. Michelsen (San Diego, CA: ACS Publications, 1978); and *The International Atlas*, compiled and programmed by Thomas G. Shanks (San Diego, CA: ACS Publications, 1985).

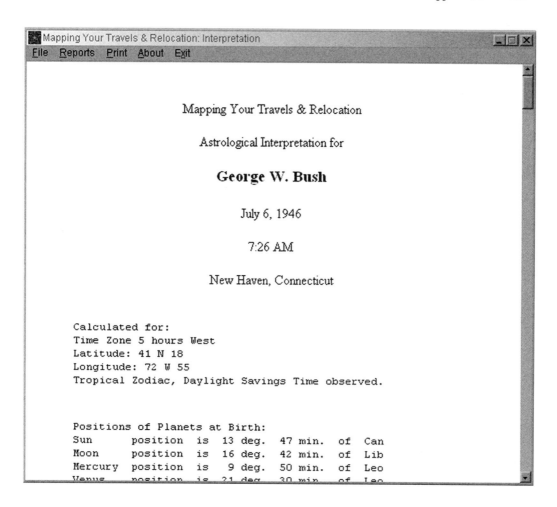

You will see George W. Bush's name and birth data, plus more information lists, and finally the interpretation for the new location you selected. To print this interpretation, click on the Print menu and select "Print."

If you select "Natal Wheel" from the Reports menu, a chart form will appear. This is Bush's birth chart. At the upper left it is labeled "Mapping Your Travels & Relocation: Chart Wheel." This form should look just like the one pictured here. If you choose "Relocated Wheel" from the Reports menu, you will see a new chart for the location you selected. To print the chart, click on the Print menu and select "Print." Only the item on the screen will print. You can choose "Interpretation" to go back to the the report.

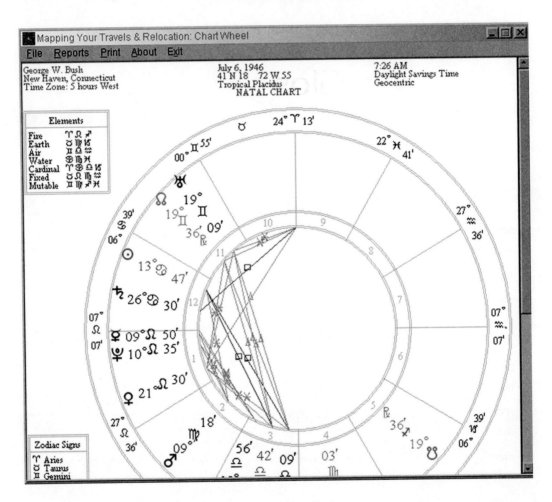

To obtain a chart and interpretation for a new location, select "Change Location for Report" from the File menu. To start over, choose "Clear All Entries and Start New List."

To go back to the opening screen, click on the Exit menu and select "Yes: Exit to Opening Screen." From here you can either exit the program by clicking on the Quit menu and selecting "Yes," or you can click on the Start menu to make another chart and interpretation.

Glossary

angle(s): The Ascendant, Descendant, Midheaven, and IC *(Imum Coeli).*

Ascendant: The first-house cusp. It represents the individual and his or her outward expression of personality.

aspect: A geometric angle that connects the energy of two or more planets.

conjunction: A major hard or soft aspect (depending upon the planets involved) where two or more planets are close to each other in the zodiac. A keyword for the conjunction is *intensity.*

degree: The zodiac has 360° and each sign has 30°. Degrees identify the position of a planet within a sign.

Descendant: The seventh-house cusp, which represents marriage and other close relationships and partnerships.

element: Each of the twelve signs is classified according to one of the four elements: fire, earth, air, or water.

hard aspect: The square, opposition, inconjunct, and conjunction (depending upon the planets in the conjunction). Hard aspects are associated with conflict and action.

house: One of the twelve pie-shaped sections (houses) of the horoscope. Each house governs specific areas of life.

house cusp: The sign and degree of the zodiac at which a house begins.

IC (Imum Coeli): The fourth-house cusp. It represents home, family, and parents.

inconjunct: A hard aspect where two or more planets are 150° apart. It indicates separation, strain, and uneasiness, because it is difficult to mix the energies of the planets involved.

intercepted sign: A zodiac sign that is contained wholly within a house and thus is not on a house cusp.

latitude: The distance in degrees north or south of the equator, which is 0° latitude. Used along with longitude to define a geographic location.

longitude: The distance in degrees east or west of Greenwich, England, which is 0° longitude. Used along with latitude to define a geographic location.

Midheaven: The tenth-house cusp. It represents career and status.

mode: Each of the twelve signs is identified with one of the three modes of expression: cardinal, fixed, or mutable.

opposition: A major action aspect where two or more planets are 180° apart, or opposite each other. This aspect represents separation and the need for compromise.

orb: The allowable distance between two or more planets that puts them in aspect to one another. The closer the aspect, the stronger its influence.

relocated chart: A birth chart calculated for a location different from the place of birth.

rulership: Each planet has rulership over, or is associated with, one (or two) signs, and the planet that rules the sign on a house cusp rules that house. The planets ruling other signs in a house are called co-rulers. Planets and signs also have natural rulership over specific areas of life, such as career, health, family, and money.

sextile: A major background aspect where two or more planets are 60° apart. This aspect represents opportunity.

soft aspect: The trine, sextile, and conjunction (depending upon the planets in the conjunction). Matters associated with soft aspects flow smoothly, but these aspects do not prompt action.

square: A major action aspect where two or more planets are 90° apart. This aspect represents action and conflict.

trine: A major background aspect where two or more planets are 120° apart. This aspect represents ease and luck.

LLEWELLYN ORDERING INFORMATION

Order Online:
Visit our website at www.llewellyn.com, select your books, and order them on our secure server.

Order by Phone:
- Call toll-free within the U.S. at 1-877-NEW-WRLD (1-877-639-9753). Call toll-free within Canada at 1-866-NEW-WRLD (1-866-639-9753)
- We accept VISA, MasterCard, and American Express

Order by Mail:
Send the full price of your order (MN residents add 7% sales tax) in U.S. funds, plus postage & handling to:

Llewellyn Worldwide
2143 Wooddale Drive, Dept. 0-7387-0665-6
Woodbury, MN 55125-2989, U.S.A.

Postage & Handling:

Standard (U.S., Mexico, & Canada). If your order is:
$49.99 and under, add $3.00
$50.00 and over, FREE STANDARD SHIPPING

AK, HI, PR: $15.00 for one book plus $1.00 for each additional book.

International Orders (airmail only):
$16.00 for one book plus $3.00 for each additional book

Orders are processed within 2 business days. Please allow for normal shipping time.
Postage and handling rates subject to change.

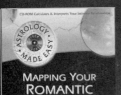